The Spirit World

An abridgement of
*"The Bible,
the Supernatural,
and the Jews"*
by

McCandlish Phillips

While this book is designed to be read for individual enjoyment and instruction, it also is intended for group study. A leader's guide is available for 95¢ from your Christian bookstore or the publisher.

Published by

VICTOR BOOKS

a division of SP Publications, Inc.
P.O. Box 1825 • Wheaton, Ill. 60187

The author and publisher gratefully acknowledge permission to reprint the following:

Excerpts from Frank S. Boshold, *Blumhardt's Battle: A Conflict with Satan.* © 1970 by Frank S. Boshold.

Excerpts from the article "Pay Now, Kill Later," *Newsweek*, October 18, 1965. © Newsweek, Inc., 1965.

Excerpts from the article "Sirhan Through the Looking Glass," reprinted by permission from *Time*, The Weekly Newsmagazine; © Time, Inc., 1969.

Excerpts from *Mademoiselle*, "Special Magical Mystery Issue." © 1968 by The Conde Nast Publications, Inc.

Excerpts from Martin Ebon, "Prophecy In Our Time" © 1968 by Martin Ebon.

Excerpts from Mary Barnard, *The Mythmakers.* © 1966 by Ohio University Press.

Excerpts from R. Gordon Wasson, "The Hallucinogenic Fungi of Mexico." Courtesy of the author.

Excerpts from Dudley Young, "The Magic of Peyote," *The New York Times Book Review*, September 29, 1968. © 1968 by The New York Times Company. Reprinted by permission.

Excerpts from Frederick Swain, "The Mystical Mushroom," reprinted from *Tomorrow*, Autumn, 1962, now *Studies in Comparative Religion*, Pates Manor, Bedfont, Middlesex, England.

Scripture quotations are from the *New American Standard Bible* (NAS) copyrighted by the Lockman Foundation, and *The Living Bible* (LB) copyrighted by Tyndale House. Other Scripture texts are from the Authorized Version. For greatest clarity the author has at certain points slightly reworded the Authorized Version, as in changing "thee" to "you," etc.

Third printing, 1974

ISBN 0-88207-048-7
Library of Congress Catalog Number 72-77015

Printed in the United States of America

For
Hannah Lowe
of Bogota,
Colombia
Faithful missionary
to whom I am indebted
beyond my knowledge

CONTENTS

Chapter 1

Demons on the Prowl

Supernaturalism in many forms has been flooding in upon the American culture in recent months, creating a sudden and widespread interest in clairvoyance, psychicism, necromancy, occultism, witchcraft, out-of-body travel, transcendental meditation, extrasensory perception, precognition, and various forms of mysticism, fetishism, spiritism. New as they may seem to the American consciousness, they are ancient supernatural practices that have found expressions in many cultures at various times in history.

If you would not thrust your hand into a snake pit, you should not permit yourself to be drawn into an involvement with one or another form of occultism, even in a tentative and purely experimental way, without knowing that it is possible for you to step over a threshold and past a door that will slam shut behind you as soon as you stand on the far side of it—slam shut so tight that nothing you can do can ever get that door open again.

That does happen. I have seen it happen. I have been told by others that something like this was happening to them but that somehow, somehow they got out of it in time. I have heard from the lips of still others that they wish that they had never become involved in what they are in, but they say that they are helpless to do anything about it now. For them there is *no exit*.

The supernatural is a tremendously potent realm. A person may pull what looks to be a small trigger and find that he has set off what for him proves to be a kind of nuclear fission of the human psyche. The powers released are far, far beyond his capacity to handle.

Throughout this book I will be discussing the visible and the invisible realms or "worlds." The first is natural. The second is supernatural. The two realms are closely inter-related. Both are populated by active, intelligent, purposeful beings.

The Bible, a book that pierces beyond the natural to the supernatural, tells us that man is set "a little lower than the angels" in the great scheme of creation. The angels are a vast company—and they are a divided company! Some serve and worship God and do His will. Others are in rebellion against God. The Scriptures speak, in Matthew 25:41, of "the devil and his angels."

The angels who serve God and the demons who follow Satan are in conflict. In the book of The Revelation we read: "Then there was war in heaven; Michael and the angels under his command fought the Dragon and his hosts of fallen angels" (Revelation 12:7, LB). The Dragon is a figurative term for Satan, the "one deceiving the whole world," as the next verse states. So we see two camps and two commanders! Michael, an archangel, is a leader of the angels of God, while Satan leads the angels now more often called demons.

There are events occurring on the earth in our generation that are affected not only by what men do and say in the natural realm but by invisible forces that are operating in the supernatural realm. The Bible reveals that the primary initiative in certain events of history does not proceed from the will of man but from the will of powers beyond man in the supernatural. Since some of these powers are evil, it is urgent to know something about them and about how they work.

Satan and his demons have access to this earth and to man. They work incessantly to draw men away from God and truth to what is evil. Their work is more widespread by far than is generally realized, affecting millions of men of every station over the whole earth. In the more extreme cases, as the Bible plainly declares, demons gain control over certain individuals.

Intelligent, invisible spiritual forces at work today select particular individuals and seek to lure them into the supernatural. These forces have an entire program or path of spiritual ruination laid out for an individual, including events that seem "providential," and the individual who begins on that path is unwittingly cooperating in a program for his own destruction.

These spiritual forces are now massively at work in North America, multiplying and spreading the means that are useful to them in hooking individuals on supernaturalism. In doing that, they are also working to subvert parts of the American culture by thoroughly infiltrating it with a broad variety of corrupt and dangerous supernatural practices.

It is no accident—it is a program—that suddenly the motion pictures, the national magazines, the bookstores and book stands are heavily freighted with graphic accounts of various adventures in supernaturalism. These accounts succeed in introducing supernaturalism into the consciousness of millions of people. For some it is only a brush, a matter of passing curiosity. Upon others it exerts the almost irresistible magnetism of a deep fascination.

They feel themselves being drawn into new levels of experience. They are aware that a force is being exerted upon their souls to draw them on into places where they have not been before, into explorations of the supernatural, into the discovery of strange new powers.

A few months ago I met a college sophomore, a bright, alert young man, quick of mind and quick of step and engagingly personable. In the course of a brief conversation he told me that his college-age brother had recently died in an automobile accident. Three weeks later he sought me out and said, with a kind of taut urgency, "I've got to talk to you." He said he had "just happened" to see a copy of a magazine lying on a desk, that he picked it up and read an account of a man's supposed contact with his dead son through a medium.

That night, he said, he took a walk around his new neighborhood and he "just happened" to see the upstairs shop of an occult reader and adviser. "I just felt drawn," he said, "strongly drawn to go up there," to ask her if she could put him into contact with his dead brother. What excited him particularly, he said, was that an alleged "sign" of such contact—milk going sour too soon—spoken of in the magazine article had also occurred to him.

There it was—two coincidences and a strangely compelling urge, and this young man was on the verge of getting involved in things against which the Bible gives the most clear-cut warnings. Without knowing it in any way, he was beginning to fall into a carefully arranged trap. I opened the Bible and showed him several passages directly bearing on the very thing he was slipping into. After he had read them he said, "I won't go near that place again."

This book is not a condemnation of everything

supernatural. There is a hunger and a longing in man for contact with something above and beyond him, something that is eternal and sure. There is a human need for supernatural experience, a deep and legitimate need. Some, out of ignorance or prejudice, may deny the supernatural and scoff at it. I do not. I know that it is real.

Everyone knows that there are fakers and gyp artists and charlatans among those who deal in the supernatural realm, but there are also individuals who do in fact possess certain powers and who are able to exercise them and to produce results by them, if not always, sometimes. The fakers can do you no good; the others may do you great harm.

For those who do exercise supernatural powers, the right question is not whether their powers are real. The right question is: Where, exactly where, do they obtain those powers?

Supernaturalism has come into this country in a rush and it is here to stay, whether we like it or not. Wearing blinders will not help. Americans need desperately to know what the Bible says about it, before tragedy strikes homes and families who don't know what is happening to their young members, or why.

The Bible is a safe, sure guide to the supernatural. It distinguishes sharply and adamantly between two enormously potent supernatural realms, as between two irreconcilable forces. These two are in conflict, in the earth and in the heavens. As to their effect upon the earth—which of them shall prevail in human affairs in this generation—man must choose.

A Victim of Magic

Cases of demon-controlled persons show a remarkable consistency whenever and wherever they occur.

A missionary to Europe and a former missionary to China, neither of whom knew anything of the other's experiences, gave me accounts of their dealings with demon-controlled individuals that matched in point after point. And these accounts were consistent, even in some of their least ordinary details, with many others that I read about or heard or saw at first hand.

The pattern of tremendous consistency that ran through account after account reflects the supernatural reality separately encountered by many individuals, widely scattered in place and time. Demons are about the same in their manifestations wherever and whenever they are found. Their powers are used against their victims in ways that have remained the same throughout human history.

A friend of mine, Frank S. Boshold, recently completed a translation into English of an extraordinary document: an account by a German Lutheran minister of his harrowing, and ultimately successful, effort to bring relief to a demon-possessed parishioner.

The account, made by the minister as his official report to the Synod of Württemberg, was later published in Germany under the title *Blumhardts Kampf*. It is now available in English under the title *Blumhardt's Battle: A Conflict With Satan*. I have permission to quote portions that show the range of effects that may be suffered in an extremely serious case of molestation by evil spirits.

The writer is Johann Christoph Blumhardt (1805–1880). The victim for whom relief was sought was Gottliebin Dittus. The events described occurred in 1842 and 1843 in Möttlingen, Germany.

"When she [Gottliebin] prayed at the table . . . she had a fit in which she fell to the floor, unconscious. What was heard was a frequently recurring trampling and scuffing in the bedroom, the living room, and the kitchen. At times these noises lasted all night. . . .

"I decided to make an investigation in the house. I made a secret agreement with the mayor of the town, carpet manufacturer Kraushaar, a sensible, sober, and God-fearing man; and several men of the town council. [We] arrived, unexpected, around 10 o'clock in the evening. . . . As soon as I entered the living room, two immense bangs met me from the bedroom. In a short time, others followed. Noises, bangs, and knockings of the most varied kind were heard, mostly in the bedroom, where Gottliebin lay on her bed, fully dressed. . . . Everything was checked in greatest detail but no explanation could be found in any wise . . . as soon as something was heard she usually would fall into violent convulsions. . . .

"On a Sunday night I went there again when a number of her women friends were present and silently watched her terrible convulsions. . . .

"It hurt me to think that there should be no means of help in such a horrible affair. . . . I jumped forward, took her stiff hands, pulled her fingers together with force as for prayer, loudly spoke her name into her ear in her unconscious state and said, 'Fold your hands and pray, "Lord Jesus, help me!" *We have seen long enough what the devil is doing, now we also want to see what Jesus can do.*' After a few moments she awakened, prayed those words after me, and all convulsions ceased, to the great surprise of those present. This was the decisive moment which pulled me into activity for the cause with irresistible power. Before, I had not the slightest thought of it."

Pastor Blumhardt, having seen that the case lay

beyond the power of physicians to relieve, took the matter on at the level on which it actually was—the level of supernatural conflict. Almost immediately, he became the object of counterattack.

He found that "something hostile in her was directing itself against me. . . . She clenched her fists, . . . close to my eyes as if she wanted to rip out both of my eyes quickly. . . . Finally the whole thing passed when with great force she thrashed repeatedly. . . .

"She tore her hair, banged her head against the wall, and tried to hurt herself in many ways." She narrowly survived two attempts at suicide.

As to why Gottliebin Dittus had become so victimized by evil spirits, the minister traced the influence of witchcraft back to her earliest childhood. A relative tried to inculcate her in magic as a small girl. Magic means and magic medications were used on her when she was sick. She had been marked for involvement in magic, but having been instructed in faith in the living God, the girl struggled vainly to keep away from its grip. "She felt herself bound to one side, the Satanic, with a certain power and her heart sought for the other side, the divine."

In the battle, Pastor Blumhardt found that he could prevail over the forces of darkness that had claimed her only by employing what he called "the honest weapons of spiritual warfare," prayer and fasting.

The minister cast out 14 demons on one occasion. "After those 14 demons were expelled, the number climbed quickly to 175 then to 425," he wrote.

"During the course of the following days it became evident that by far not all the demons had been removed from the patient. . . . She would often lie as dead while her breath was held from within her. . . . Also sometimes she was so paralyzed that she could hardly move a member of her body by her own will. . . . With other spirits which identified themselves from then on, there seemed to be a question of what was going to happen to them. . . . They had a terror of the abyss which they felt near now and said, among other things, 'You are our worst enemy, but we, too, are your enemies. If only we could as we would!' And then again, 'Oh, if only there were no God in heaven!' . . . The patient was tortured incessantly. Her body would often swell extraordinarily and she would vomit. . . . She also received frequent blows on her head, knocks in the side, and in addition suffered from heavy nose-bleeding. . . ."

The desired end of the story came in late December 1843 when everything that had happened before seemed to come together once more. After an especially intensive seige upon Gottliebin, as well as upon her sister and a half-blind brother, the demons left, never to return. "At 2 o'clock in the morning . . . ," according to Pastor Blumhardt, "the girl bent back her head and upper part of her body over the backrest of the chair, with a voice of which one could hardly have believed a human throat capable, [and cried] 'Jesus is Victor! Jesus is Victor!' —words that sounded so far and were understood at such a distance that they made an unforgettable impression on many people.

". . . That was the point at which the battle of two years came to an end . . . she slowly came to complete health. All her former illnesses which are well known to the doctors were completely healed . . . her health became ever stronger and more durable. [Gottliebin Dittus became a teacher of children marked by] insight, love, patience, and kindness . . . . Now that a school for small children is to be built, I cannot find a person who would be as suitable as she to lead this school."

Six years later, Pastor Blumhardt wrote of her continued stability, health, and usefulness.

A Modern Victim of Magic

In the months before he fatally wounded Robert F. Kennedy, Sirhan Sirhan steeped himself in the lore of occultism and magic. The assassin's prolonged experimentation with mysticism, and his use of a mirror, was detailed in the long aftermath of that jarring event.

In his bedroom, Sirhan spent scores of hours reading about the Middle East and the occult. He described about 20 books he read during the year preceding the slaying, dealing with metaphysics and the power of the mind.

In an article titled "Sirhan Through the Looking Glass," *Time* reported: "A mirror. Two flickering candles. And Sirhan Sirhan. Alone in his cramped room, day after day, hour after silent hour, Sirhan studied Sirhan. Mail order courses in Rosicrucian mysticism had given him a new creed. They told the disturbed Christian Arab that he could unlock from the mirror image of Sirhan Sirhan the inner knowledge, happiness, and power he craved.

"Once, instead of his own image in the mirror, Sirhan saw a vision of Robert Kennedy, the man he was soon afterward to kill.

"The candles swayed and changed color. . . . One key to the killing," according to the psychoanalyst, Dr. Bernard L. Diamond, "must be found in Sirhan's arcane experiments with the mirror. It was during his self-induced trances, Diamond said, that Sirhan scribbled over and over that 'Kennedy must die.'"

It would seem probable that, through the devices and rituals of magic, Sirhan unknowingly incurred an alliance with demons who were able to drive him to apparent insanity and to murder. His private aberration had public consequences that cut close to the very heart of national life in the United States.

Witchcraft in America

There has nearly always been a certain amount of spiritualism, possibly also of witchcraft, practiced in the United States, but for the most part it has been off in remote and obscure corners of our national life and has rarely enjoyed widespread public favor. Lately, however, we have watched a rising vogue in occultism, astrology, magic, the work of mediums, witchcraft, and the like.

Accounts have appeared in newspapers, magazines, and books in the last two years in which persons who practice some form of witchcraft have told of their activities. The *Daily News*, the New York tabloid newspaper with the largest circulation in the nation, carried a full-page story by Lisa Hoffman about a witchcraft cult on Long Island, from which I quote in part:

"Don't make the mistake of thinking all this is a piece of arcane flummery. Twentieth-century witches are deadly serious. The chants, the swords, the music, the symbols, the herbs, and the incense are all pretty much what they were in the pre-Christian era of nature cults, when the bizarre practice was born."

Mademoiselle magazine made witchcraft the theme of a "Special Magical Mystery Issue." The cover promised: "Sorcery and Sex: A terrific tour of spells, charms, witchcraft, and the mysterious East

. . . Yoga . . . India's exciting Tantric art. Chilling occult novel complete in this issue."

The issue included an interview with Dr. Harry E. Wedeck, a college professor with an extensive knowledge of the history of witchcraft.

"It's old. It's all so old," Dr. Wedeck said, observing that he had recently read *Chin P'ing Mei,* a book translated from a sixteenth-century manuscript, which mentioned "witchcraft practices, astrological lore, and spells that were precisely those found in Theocritus and Vergil."

"Vergil to a sixteenth-century Chinese text— that's quite a jump isn't it?" the interviewer said, to which the scholar gave this significant reply: "These beliefs are so pervasive that I feel they are not necessarily transmitted one to the other, but develop independently."

It is important to catch the essence of that. It appears that these practices are *not transmitted* from culture to culture, but that they have sprung up spontaneously and independently. The fact is that these practices have their origin outside of the mind of man in a single supernatural source: Satan.

Such practices are expressions of his religious purposes for mankind, and he transmits them directly from the spiritual realm into the human realm. Demons have access to every culture and it is in their power to communicate mysteries of Satan to individuals in each.

That these practices are so often identical in culture after culture between which there has been no human communication is an evidence of their supernatural origin and design. The same bizarre religious ceremonies and costumes have been found among remote tribes in Africa, in the far Pacific and in South America.

Time magazine did a cover story on the many

eruptions of occultism in the American culture. Sybil Leek's *Diary of a Witch* was extensively reviewed in the mass media.

Public interest in such matters is rising, so much so that according to a report in *The New York Times:* "Harvard University's Coop, a huge merchandising mart on Harvard Square, recently opened a paperback book section for books on the occult. . . . Mr. [Roscoe] Fitts said that there had been an increase in interest in the occult, extrasensory perception, fortune-telling, numerology, and mind-expansion drugs in the last six months, enough to set up a new section that includes titles on witchcraft."

This is not an isolated phenomenon. It is becoming a national one, and the curiosity about such things runs highest among the young.

Witchcraft and magic, in spite of their widely assumed nonexistence, are suddenly and prominently with us today. These things have not thronged upon the scene by any mere coincidence. They are timed and carefully planned for the weakening of the society and the damaging of thousands in it, and they will increase rapidly among the people. They will only be reversed if there is an awareness of their source and an awakening to faith in the living God. The present tragedy of America is that it has long left the truths of the scriptural faith on which many of its founders stood, and to which a majority of the people at least gave assent. That is why America has lost its way.

In domestic and international affairs the nation staggers as if it is drunk. Its incapacity to devise effective policies is a reflection of the fact that the nation has cast aside the truth and has gone after lies. The lies that people show themselves willing to swallow get bigger every year.

Some young people are rushed into the demonic supernatural with startling speed. A friend told me a week ago of a young man he knows at work who participated in an experiment in group occultism. During the exercise he suddenly found himself set in a weird scene, as by a vision: He was walking in a long corridor between two rows of Buddha statues that were alive. This frightened him. He broke the spell and came back into reality. Almost immediately he had a different experience. He felt himself turned into a snake. He described in vivid detail the sensation he experienced as a snake. He had no physical change, of course, but his perception of himself was transformed by demons who were able to take him over, at least temporarily, because of his participation in the occult exercise. Such group occult practices can conduct people directly into the realm of the demons.

Occultism and idolatry go together.

Those who practice spiritism, so-called transcendental meditation, various kinds of mysticism, the black arts, magic, communication with the dead, psychicism, witchcraft, and many other kinds of demonic supernaturalism commonly use idols and other religious objects in their practices. All of this, whatever name it may bear, whatever guise it may wear, is satanic in its origin and is directly opposed to the clear teaching of the Bible.

"You shall not . . . practice divination or soothsaying. . . . Do not turn to mediums or spiritists; do not seek them out to be defiled by them. I am the Lord your God" (Leviticus 19:26b, 31, NAS).

"There shall not be found among you anyone who makes his son or his daughter pass through the fire, *one who uses divination, one who practices witchcraft, or one who interprets omens, or a sorcerer, or one who casts a spell, or a medium, or a spiritist, or one who calls up the dead.* For whoever does these things is detestable to the Lord" (Deuteronomy 18:10-12a, NAS).

The ancient practices of occultism, divination, witchcraft, and false worship have not improved with age, nor have they changed much. And the Word of God still stands against them, because they are the work of an enemy.

New Gods Rush In

In the Old Testament Book of Judges there is a compelling assertion that says:

"New gods were chosen; then war was in the gates" (Judges 5:8, NAS).

New gods are swarming into the American culture. Gods that were never heretofore present in the nation are coming in. For that reason there is spiritual warfare at the gates of the nation and the destiny of the United States will depend on whether the people choose to honor God or to honor the gods. There is no true god but the God of Israel, the God of the Bible. Each of the "gods" is a demon spirit.

In the song of Moses, the leader of Israel remembered how the true God had encircled and cared for Israel and "guarded him as the pupil of His eye . . . the Lord alone guided him, and there was no foreign god with him." Later the nation "grew . . . fat, thick, and sleek—then he forsook God who made him, and scorned the Rock of his salvation. They made Him jealous with strange gods. . . .

"They sacrificed to demons who were not God, to . . . new gods who came lately, whom your fathers did not dread" (Deuteronomy 32:10b, 12, 15b, 16a, 17, NAS).

It may be said of the United States that from before its founding and through a majority of its decades one God—the God of Israel—was worshiped within its borders. The religions of the nation were Christianity and Judaism and both proclaim the God of Israel as the Creator. There were no other gods among us.

Now we have an altered situation with "strange gods . . . demons who . . . [are] not God, new gods who came lately."

Satanic forces do not have equal access to all areas of the world. In some areas the activity of evil spirits is far more prevalent and pronounced. There are regions in which Satan and his demons have had much more influence, precisely because of the extent of idolatry and false religion and occultism in those places.

God recognizes distinct entities called nations, and the Scriptures declare that He has determined the times allotted to them and the boundaries of their habitation (Acts 17:26). God deals with these geographic and political entities as nations—and so also does Satan.

Where the true God is obeyed and worshiped, blessings flow upon the people and Satan is greatly hindered in his influence upon them. Fidelity to God and to His Word breaks the power of evil spirits and erects barriers to Satan. This can be true in a life, in a home, in a nation.

Satan once complained to God that he could not get at a just man named Job to harm him because God had put a protective "hedge about him and his house and all that he has on every side."

It is possible for a nation, also, to have demon barriers surrounding it, invisible but powerful, past which demons cannot come. Those barriers are established by God. But they depend on the obedience of the people.

While the people of the United States honored the God of Israel, and gave worship to Him, while they widely accepted the standards of the Bible as the standards of public behavior, the nation enjoyed a very high degree of protection from demonic activity.

The first step in the satanic takeover of a nation is to draw the people away from faith in God and in His Word. The next stage is to increase them steadily in the indulgence of sin. The third stage is to lead them into false worship and false supernaturalism. The final stage is usually to bring them under dictatorship. We are in the third stage now.

This nation's rising indulgence in idolatry, false Eastern religions, occultism and spiritualism, and immorality gives Satan the occasion he needs to loose more and more demons upon the population.

It is not God's will that a people be overrun by demons. It is His will that a people look to Him, refuse and reject all of the devices and lies of Satan, and enjoy divine protection against the works of the devil. To keep the barriers to Satan up, there must be vigorous obedience to God and vigorous resistance to Satan. When a people have these, new gods cannot enter the gates of a nation.

On August 25, 1926, the liner *Majestic* steamed into New York harbor with a young man and an old woman aboard. The young Hindu, Jiddu Krishnamurti, a 29-year-old Brahmin born at Madanapalle, India, was being brought to the United States by Mrs. Annie Besant, 80-year-old head of the international Theosophical Society, who had discovered him, reared him, and then announced him to be the chosen vehicle through which the great "World Teacher" would again speak to mankind.

"America is ready to listen," Mrs. Besant declared on the morning of the pair's arrival. "Krishnamurti," she announced, "is the leader of the new civilization."

Krishnamurti was no less direct. "I hope," he said, "to make radical changes in America's religious life. I hope for a new civilization with my coming.

"I do not," he said, "preach repentance or the remission of sins."

In 1909, Mrs. Besant had begun the preparation of Krishnamurti for use by the World Teacher, or "Guiding Spirit of the Universe"—described as the invisible head of every religion. She asserted that "when the World Teacher manifests himself he takes possession of Mr. Krishnamurti's body." Krishnamurti's mission, she said, was to combine all religions into one new, worldwide religion, uniting mankind in brotherhood.

In 1911, a supernatural sign seemed to confirm Krishnamurti's future role when "a great coronet of brilliant shimmering blue appeared above his head" to members of the Order of the Star in the East, founded by Mrs. Besant. On Dec. 28, 1925, in a grove at Adyar, 6,000 delegates from many nations heard Krishnamurti. Near the end of his address, he broke off, and "then another voice, a voice of wondrous sweetness and power, rang out through his lips," and Krishnamurti spoke in the first person as a god. Some of the delegates "bowed down to worship him," a news report said.

Then, in 1926, Mrs. Besant decided the time was ripe to bring her protege to America.

By the time of his arrival a good deal of excitement had been generated. A series of news reports cabled from Europe had been splashed at length in most New York newspapers.

In London, eyewitnesses gave accounts of "the apparent possession by a spirit of J. Krishnamurti." A retired British Army officer told a reporter that a group of 2,000 persons felt an impulse to adoration as they listened to the young man speak. A physicist said he saw "a huge star over Krishnamurti's head burst into fragments and come raining down" on the slender Hindu.

On August 21 the *Evening Post* in New York observed, "No healer of the spirit, communer with the occult, or teacher of a new religion ever has come to America with the way so well paved for him as Krishnamurti."

It was at the very point of entering the gates of this nation that the whole, elaborate demonic production centered on Krishnamurti began to fall apart. Even while on shipboard in New York harbor, Krishnamurti complained of what he called the electrical atmospheric intensity of New York and said he doubted that he would be able to meditate successfully there.

"During an interview session at the pier, the atmospheric intensity affected him to the degree that "he became so excited as to reach the stage of incoherence." *The New York Times* reported, "The 'holy man' proved to be a shy, badly frightened, nice-looking young Hindu."

On coming into the nation, Krishnamurti encountered a spiritual resistance great enough to make him doubtful of his mission. There was something in the air, invisible but powerful, that stood against him. Plans for him to speak in a public appearance in New York were canceled. The next day, Mrs. Besant explained that Krishnamurti had not yet come into full possession of his powers. His body had been "visited," she said, but not "possessed." Stripped of certain powers and also of certain demonic signs that had worked for him in India and in Europe, Krishnamurti appeared now to be nothing more than a genteel young man giving a few innocuous opinions to newsmen who interviewed him.

Krishnamurti was taken directly to Chicago for a convention of Theosophists and the city made him surprisingly snappish. Told by newsmen that his visit had proved to be a disappointment, he complained of *bad atmospheric conditions* prevailing in this country. "It is no wonder that nothing has happened," he said. Those conditions rendered him helpless to show the supernatural effects, that, in other nations, had seemed to confirm his mission, both to his followers and to himself.

Plans for a national tour were set aside. The young Hindu went into seclusion and quickly faded from public view as a miracle man. In 1929, Mrs. Besant was greatly distressed when Krishnamurti flatly renounced all the pretensions that had surrounded his messianic role. He had been a victim of them as much as anybody, but the spiritual conditions then prevailing in this country enabled him to come out from under his terrible delusion.

The demons behind the Krishnamurti affair could not at that time break through the invisible barrier that God had set around this nation against the spirits of the East, their false doctrines, and their counterfeit miracles. There were to be no new gods in the gates of America then.

But within some 40 years demons would prowl freely in America. Had his visit come in recent years, Krishnamurti would have been quite comfortable—even as the Maharishi Yogi was when he entered the United States for a visit that proved an immediate and rousing public success.

Chapter 2

Marching to
Satan's Music

A witch appeared on Wall Street in the spring of 1970. For a few minutes at the lunch hour she practiced an element of magic there. Not long afterward Wall Street became the scene of mob disruptions.

It was on Friday, March 13, that a young woman who works in public relations in New York arranged for the witch to appear on Wall Street near Broad Street in downtown Manhattan to "cast a spell of sexual vitality over Wall Street," as it was put.

Workers on lunch hour crowded around the visitor, who persuaded them to join her in chanting, "Light the flame, bright the fire, red is the color of desire." They unified their voices in that old staple of witchcraft, an incantation to stir passion. A spell was cast, and a curse went into effect.

It was at Wall Street near Broad Street on Friday, May 8 of the same year, that a mob of 300 or more men in hard hats, mostly construction workers, stormed into the financial district behind a cluster of American flags and attacked student protestors who had gathered on the steps of Federal Hall, where George Washington took the presidential oath of office in 1789.

Gangs of men ran through the narrow streets of the financial district, beating and kicking young people as well as other bystanders to whom they objected, including a couple of lawyers whose hair was not short enough to suit them. Some of the men carried heavy, small construction tools. They shouted things like "Kill the Commies" and, while they carried out their brief terroristic rampage, several thousand pedestrians loudly cheered their fist and boot assaults. About seventy persons were injured. When a first aid station was set up in nearby Trinity Church, the angry workers tore a Red Cross banner from the church gates.

This was all done in the good name of patriotism, but it was the crudest kind of mob action. It was the beginning of an overt right-wing response to overt left-wing radicalism.

I watched news films later. The men had paraded down Broadway. When they reached Wall and Broad, their lines suddenly broke from a march to the headlong disorder of a running mob.

As it happened, the disintegration of the march into a violent outbreak began within yards of the point at which the spell of witchcraft had been cast. The division that exists in a more and more polarized citizenry broke out there that day in street clashes.

It is not possible to trace the relationship between these two events, and therefore nothing dogmatic can be asserted about it. What can be said is that witchcraft and magic are related to the work of demons. They are acts of human cooperation with evil spirits. Such acts may affect events to a degree that is little understood.

It is perhaps more than a mere coincidence that witchcraft had come to that Wall Street scene first. I do not suggest that those who practiced an aspect of witchcraft there had any intention whatever of creating a spiritual disturbance. The witch, who sought only to draw attention to herself, succeeded in getting a fairly large number of bystanders to join her in uttering an occult incantation. Such chants are a call to demons, whether the persons who utter them intend them to be so or not.

There is no necessary relation between what is *intended* in acts of witchcraft and false worship and what is actually brought about by them. Burning incense to other gods, during the time of Jeremiah, was intended to procure some kind of favor or good fortune; it brought the desolation of Jerusalem (Jeremiah 44:1-6a).

The rule, rarely excepted, is that *spiritual* transgression precedes the physical manifestations that are its visible result. If spiritual laws are broken or ignored, certain effects will inevitably succeed.

Early in the rise of Hitler and Nazism in Germany, occultist elements were actively in play. They were not always openly shown, but a bold clairvoyant named Erik Jan Hanussen, a dealer in astrology and in predicting future events, became known as the "Prophet of the Third Reich."

In the book *Prophecy in Our Time,* Martin Ebon writes that "in the midst of the political churnings, with violence permeating the air of the German capital, Hanussen went on ahead with the opening of his lavish 'Palace of the Occult,' taking up an entire floor at fashionable No. 16, Lietzenstrasse." It was filled with "magical paraphernalia. . . . Golden signs of the Zodiac looked down upon broad, low couches."

At the opening, with "actors and actresses mingling with Nazi bigwigs . . . the 'Prophet of the Third Reich' took his place in the center of his lit-up glass circle; everything else was thrown into darkness." He described a vision "in halting, deep-throated tones of fear and menace:

"'. . . The Storm Troopers move down the Wilhemstrasse. There has been a magnificent victory. The people want Hitler. Victory, Victory! Hitler is victorious. Resistance is useless. But the noise comes closer. Is there a struggle? Shooting? No, . . . no, . . . it is not that. . . . I see flames, enormous flames. . . . It is a terrible conflagration that has broken out. Criminals have set the fire.

"'They want to hurl Germany into last-minute chaos, to nullify the victory. . . . Only the mailed fist of an awakened Germany can hold back chaos and the threat of civil war. . . .'

"That was on the 26th of February, 1933. On the evening of February 27, at about 9:30, the news-agency teletypes in London, New York, and throughout the world were reporting a flash: 'The Reichstag is burning!'

"Hanussen's spectacular prophecy had come true. With it his own flamboyant success seemed assured, especially amidst the violence that was immediately loosed; the Nazis used the Reichstag fire as an excuse to cancel the elections and embark on the reign of terror that lasted until Hitler's suicide in his Berlin underground bunker, ending World War II, a decade later."

The accuracy of a prophecy may be an indication of its supernatural origin, but it is certainly no test of divine origin. Hanussen's prophecy was apparently right, yet its purport was entirely evil.

The Scriptures warn that even when "a prophet or dreamer of dreams" gives a sign or a wonder that actually comes to pass as he said, if the spiritual content is contrary to the Word of God, the prophet is a deceiver. "You shall follow the Lord your God and fear Him; and you shall keep His commandments, [and] listen to His voice" above the words of all such prophets (see Deuteronomy 13:1-4, NAS).

At the time of the convulsive events by which Russia was to be conveyed from one form of tyranny to another and still bloodier form, the mad monk Rasputin moved to the nerve centers of power and manipulated events with skill, daring, and considerable cunning. He used occult powers to gain decisive influence on the Czarist' side. Statesmen who stood against him lost their positions, and he put feeble and corrupt lackeys into their places.

It is well to remember that liberty, once it is lost, may remain wholly out of reach for a long time. Nations have sometimes suffered repression and virtual enslavement for decades stretching into centuries. The psychic, occult, and spiritual forces now at work in the United States, with a large degree of public acceptance, are sufficient to plunge this nation first toward anarchy and later into the grip of a Red or a fascist tyranny.

The Media—Marching to Satan's Music

Supernatural forces of destruction are now making swift headway in undermining the welfare and sanity of many of the nation's young people, with little left to check them, and the communications media do mighty service in widely publicizing the works of Satan among the young.

One night last week, I looked up from my desk to see the distraught face of an editor before me, a man I have long known. His most prominent characteristics are precision in manner, in dress, and in the expression of thought, and a vast affection for his children. I had met his children and they had impressed me as exceptional for quickness of mind and an almost adult composure. This night he was slightly drunk. I had never seen him drunk before. He told me that his 11-year-old boy had stayed away from home for several days. It was more than a kid's lark. The boy gave his father reason to think that he might bolt from home again. Fearing that the boy might leave and have no money, he said, "All right, Son. I want you to stay, but if you go, here's five dollars for some food."

The boy's response was, "I don't want any of your establishment money."

The speech, of course, could hardly have arisen from any thought-out position. It was a kind of parroting of something the boy had heard. At some point he had come under the influence of ideas that were radically affecting his behavior.

There have sprung up in some cities skid rows for young runaways. For a while New York City's East Village became a lodestone for the young, and some of the mass media served as the lodestar to guide them to that dismal precinct. My work took me there to see haggard young people living aimlessly on bare mattresses in ratty, dirty, unfurnished flats. Some of them were out on the street begging dimes and quarters for slices of pizza to keep them going.

I remember one spring day going into a nest of revolutionary young people in a corner building for interviews. When I came out I saw entering the building, suitcase in hand, a nice-looking young kid, obviously just out of college for the summer, apparently drawn by what he had heard or read, and I wondered how long it would be before he would be in the demoralized condition some of the others were in.

Under the influence of sexual indulgence, drugs, and mysticism, young people often undergo swift transformations. You see a young person with a clear eye and a clear face, still fresh with the innocence of youth, and a few months later the freshness is gone and you see a thoroughly different person and you wonder how such great change could happen so soon.

The underground papers serve their youthful constituency an unrelieved diet of pot-sex-revolution-mysticism and psychedelic adventure and thereby spread the fashions of the youth subculture, but there are national magazines that are hardly less ardent in seeking out every new excess, even if practiced by a miniscule fraction of the population, and describing it in ample detail for millions throughout the country.

Esquire magazine assiduously digs up fresh modes of aberration among the young and gives them the full blaze of tutorial publicity, especially in its annual campus issue, published a couple of weeks before the opening of the fall college term each year, just in time to inculcate incoming freshmen in the foulest ways of campus and off-campus existence: Let the demons plant some new deviation among 1 or 2 percent of the students at half a dozen campuses, and it is soon seized and conveyed to every town and village in the nation by the media. It is hardly possible anymore for a teenager to be preserved in innocence; vile corruptions are transmitted to him by print and by film week after week after week.

In one issue *Esquire* printed a long series of side-by-side photographs of male students, showing each face before and after the effects of campus life had registered on it. The contrasts were shaking. The before pictures were of apparently mostly normal, straight young guys; the after pictures constituted a gallery of abnormalcy and degeneracy. Huge transformations had taken place in the interval between high school and college graduations.

The New York Times Magazine for January 26, 1969, carried an article by Arno Karlen reporting on

"The Unmarried Marrieds on Campus," men and women living together in "unmarried bliss," except that the author often found these illicit relationships tense and glum—anything but blissful.

His article closed with an incredible lament: These "couples" tended to stick together too exclusively in their live-together "arrangements." It isn't that there is too much sexual laxity and promiscuity, the writer proposed, it is that there is too little!

American society and its stability are beginning to break down under the hammers of violence and a revolutionary discontent, and the family is beginning to disintegrate and to give way to patterns found among cats. And as this happens, author Karlen publicly wishes that "more students were shacked up," and regrets only that there are limitations of any kind on free-lance sexual experience.

So it is that the nation's most respected newspaper allows its magazine to become the Sunday pulpit for a plea for more and looser sexual relationships among the young, and another blow is administered to the crumbling foundation of American social stability.

Misery and joylessness are the inevitable result of this demonically inspired drive to destroy family relationships and to encourage anybody to have sex with anybody anytime. This is the wisdom that the Bible describes as "earthly, sensual, devilish," and the mass media multiply it and amplify it a millionfold or more and fill the land with it.

The media are not a luxury in a free society, they are a necessity. They are the chief means by which information on just about everything of major consequence in world and national affairs is made regularly, cheaply, readily, and swiftly available to the public. Since a democracy could not function without an informed citizenry, the news media are an indispensable part of the landscape of a free society. For all their faults, the news media do a magnificent job of keeping people informed.

Again and again, however, the lowest and basest elements have been chosen as the objects of singular attention in the press. Sometimes the media seem almost to have gone to lengths to find, and expose to public view, the few that have sunk deepest in evil. A rock group known for its appallingly degenerate behavior was given a big spread in *Life*. Not long afterward, one of its members confessed puzzlement about this to a college newspaper writer, who quoted him as saying, "I don't see why they would take four mugs like us, who believe in fornication in the streets, and give us all that ink."

Moral anarchists, ideological extremists, proponents of resort to violence, and agents of the false supernatural are among the spiritual forces that contribute to the subversion of a society. There are spiritual forces that contribute to the stability and justice of a society, but the mass media direct most of the attention to the divisive and disruptive forces, while too often ignoring those that make for cohesion, stability, and a viable unity.

Too often what is happening on a rather small, but noisy and gaudy, band of the whole American spectrum is selected for public attention. Thus the media tend to present an artificially distorted, unbalanced picture of reality. The effect is rather like that of one of those peculiar fun house mirrors that enlongate or fatten certain features of what they reflect while unnaturally compressing others. Unspeakable filth and illustrated guides to sin and to demonic supernaturalism have lately spilled out onto almost every newsstand, magazine rack, and book rack, where young people can easily get them.

The Scriptures have a word for the men and

women who publish and circulate such material as this, laying Satan's snares for the feet of young people:

"Woe to the world because of its stumbling blocks!" Jesus said. "For it is inevitable that stumbling blocks come; but woe to that man through whom the stumbling block comes! It would be better for him if a millstone were hung around his neck and he were thrown into the sea, than that he should cause one of these little ones to stumble. . . . It is not the will of your Father who is in heaven that one of these little ones perish" (Matthew 18:7, 14; Luke 17:1, 2, NAS).

"It is necessary that temptations (stumbling blocks) come," Jesus said. It is necessary because Satan and the demons will see to it. "But woe to *the man* by whom the temptation comes!"

Not long after the assassination of Robert F. Kennedy, an editor for one of the nation's major publishing houses said to me, "I'm getting out of the violence business." He had decided, on the basis of too many assassinations, to stop publishing books accenting violence.

The editor took his house out of the physical violence line, because he could see the necessity of that, but he did not take his house out of the promotion of *spiritual violence*. It is spiritual violence that gives rise to various forms of physical violence. Sirhan Sirhan is a prime example of that.

The editor's house published, among other things, the story and teachings of the Maharishi Yogi and spread them in an inexpensive paperback edition across the country, where they have, of course, exerted a primary attraction on young people. A book so filled with false and demonic mysticism, contrary to the revelation of God, and contrary to the central truths of the Judeo-Christian tradition, can quickly subvert the minds of young people.

A common excuse for much of this is that it reaches them with "their own thing." In many cases it is not really "their own thing," it is Satan's thing that the media are spreading among youth.

One thing Satan and his demons are pushing on youth is revolution. Revolution exists first as a concept, as a defined goal, before it is carried into practical action. The theory of Marxism preceded the historical and geopolitical fact of Marxism, with all Russia and all China dwelling under its banners. It is not reasonable to expect that so heavy a dose of revolutionary doctrine as is now being administered to a generation of college students will not later produce a harvest of violence. There are students on campuses today who are so thoroughly swayed by these doctrines that they will live for them and die for them in the years ahead. If you trace the lives of some of the communist leaders who now rule nations, you find that they became communists as a result of ideas sown in their minds during their college years. They absorbed those ideas while in college and they have lived by them ever since.

In an article titled "Meet the Women of the Revolution," Peter Babcox wrote that "there is a quickening disposition among the young . . . that the salvation of our culture is revolution. It is an amorphous, tumultuous phenomenon, both a state of mind and an organized political force." He told of a 27-year-old woman who writes poems of revolution and quoted these lines: *"I am pregnant with murder. The pains are coming faster now."*

Why is it that from New York to San Francisco, from Michigan to Florida, everywhere in the nation among the young, these themes became so markedly prevalent? Is it just a coincidence? Or, is it a plan?

Is it just a coincidence that astrology and yogism are suddenly everywhere to be seen—on the cover of the women's service magazine at the checkout counter in the supermarket, in the window of the diet foods shop, in the advertisement that comes with the junk mail, and in many places where they confront the American mind in a novel or compelling way? Or is it a plan? Suddenly, everywhere, astrology, mysticism, Hinduism, Buddhism, occultism.

Let me assure you that I do not regard it as the work of any kind of human conspiracy whatever. The almost unlimited power, the near-omnipotence casually ascribed to human beings by some theories of conspiracy is a product of some combination of ignorance, suspicion, hate, and superstition. Such theories are fables lacking evidence. Behind such theories there is sometimes an animating desire to create human scapegoats. If it were a human conspiracy it could not appear so suddenly and run so far so fast. It simply could not be so pervasive. There is no sinister human cabal that has such limitless access to all the means of publicity and communication as these things so readily enjoy.

The Bible, in assigning blame for evil working, fixes primary attention not on men but on demon powers, not on the earth but in the atmosphere and in the heavens. It reveals that, in contending against evil, men of God "do not wrestle against flesh and blood"—that is, against other men—"but against principalities, against powers, against the rulers of the darkness of this world, against *spiritual wickedness in high places*" (Ephesians 6:12).

Many of the fads and crazes and styles and practices that are being pushed now upon the young people are demonic in origin and expressly contrary to the teachings of the Bible. Satan's policy does not change. Not only are there very evident similarities in what the demons are doing at many points in our society, but some of these things are virtually identical to what demons have done in other societies at former times in history. This is especially so in regard to gross sexual excess and public exhibition. There is nothing new about that; it has been a mark of once great societies soon to be defunct.

The major themes sounded by the underground press also run through the lyrics of popular music performed by the young for the young. The *Yale Daily News* ran a review of a record album under the headline "Stones Release Revolutionary LP." In it the same basic Satanic program—drugs, sex, occultism, and revolution—is thrust upon young people. The article begins with a quotation:

"*The time is right for palace revolution . . . the time is right for fighting in the streets.*'

"Rock music censors who banned the Rolling Stones' 'Street Fighting Man' are going to have their hands full when they hear 'Beggars Banquet,' the group's latest album.

"Six of the ten songs are blatantly revolutionary, their heavy rhythms pounding, mobilizing, appealing to the people.

"The Rolling Stones came up out of the streets, screaming their rhythm and blues to hordes of shouting teens. Songs like 'It's All Over Now' and 'Let's Spend the Night Together' precipitated many riots, yet those songs contained no attempt at lyrical mobilization as such.

"A few years ago, the Stones stopped touring. Distracted from real hard rock by their drug experiences, they produced 'Their Satanic Majesty's Request.' Many thought Mick Jagger and company were through with the hard stuff for good, in a dream world of acid and flowers.

" 'Beggars Banquet' has proved these people wrong. The Rolling Stones are definitely back in the revolutionary hard rock thing. . . . The inside cover of the album shows the Rolling Stones—hair long and bedraggled, lips painted—in a banquet scene of drunken lust and gluttony." One of the songs in the album is titled "Sympathy for the Devil."

The youth subculture is shot through with the philosophy of Satan. There is ceaseless, incessant, pounding propaganda in the ears and eyes of youth, promoting fornication, mysticism, marijuana, and violent revolution, and we are at the point where young women seek roles as "urban guerrillas" and others say they feel "pregnant with murder."

Satan and the demons have created a quagmire for young people. Now they are urging them to march into it by the masses, and they are supplying the lyrics, the drumbeat, and the tune. The media—motion pictures, records, print—are plugging it hard (with varying degrees of sophistication but with the same basic line of sin). That quagmire—with its come-ons of easy sex, drugs, supernatural experiences, and participation in revolution—is a trap. Many who venture into it, curious to see what it is like, will sink in it and will never get back out.

The Bible promises that "when the enemy comes in like a flood, the Spirit of the Lord shall lift up a standard against him" (Isaiah 59:19b) and everyone who comes to that standard will be safe from the works of the devil.

While it is true that the attack on youth is supernaturally planned, it is also true that the answer to it is supernaturally planned.

The only thing that will break the grip of the supernatural of Satan over young people today is the supernatural power of God.

Chapter 3

Journey into the Supernatural

In the creation there is a physical order and a spiritual order, both of which are real. The physical universe is natural. The spiritual order is supernatural. There are facts that may be known about both, but not by the same means.

Man's body, and the five senses that go with it, is a part of the physical creation. Those senses are able to observe and to take in information, facts, about the natural universe—and that is all. They cannot observe the supernatural order. Your senses give you your relationship to the physical universe. They are the mediators and sentinels between you and all the rest of the physical creation. You know of it and learn of it by exercising them.

There it ends. They provide you with no information about the supernatural order. They afford you no relationship to it. Your ears are deaf to it, your eyes are blind to it.

The Bible says:

The things which are seen are temporal, but the things which are not seen are eternal. (2 Corinthians 4:18b).

We give ready assent to the statement that "the things which are seen are temporal." We know that to be the fact. We are much less sure that "the things which are unseen are eternal."

Notice that the verse does not refer to ideas, to values, and concepts; it refers to *things*. It speaks of temporal things and it speaks of eternal *things*. The contrast is not between natural stuff and spiritual values, as though a man could read the verse and say, "Sure, money and clothes wear out, but love goes on forever." To say that is to spiritualize the verse falsely.

The unseen things the Scripture says are eternal are things that have objective existence. They have that existence not on the natural and physical plane but on the spiritual and supernatural plane.

The natural man, though in full possession of his physical faculties and senses, is constitutionally incapable of discovering anything on the spiritual plane. That is as true as that a standard band radio does not receive short-wave signals. The atmosphere may be charged with such signals but the standard band radio is as dead to them as the leg of a table is.

The Bible declares that the natural man does not receive spiritual truths. "They are foolishness to him, and he *cannot* understand them, because they are spiritually appraised" (1 Corinthians 2:14, NAS).

It is an easy thing to assert that if something can't be seen it is not real, does not exist. Yet visibility is not the test of existence.

Science has lately discovered that, besides matter, there is also antimatter. "Research in physics has revealed the existence of mirror-image counterparts to all the particles composing matter on this planet," a news report said. Physicists say there may be worlds, there may be galaxies made up of antimatter. Isaac Asimov suggested that "somewhere, entirely beyond our reach or observation, there may be an antiuniverse made up almost entirely of antimatter." Since that is posited in the natural realm, it should not jar our minds too much to consider the reality of the spiritual realm.

Science is able to use methods of observation to determine certain laws that apply in the natural realm, including the laws of mathematics. But there are limits upon what man can discover by the scientific method. The whole physical universe is unlimitedly open to man to explore by the exercise of his senses, directed by his intelligence, as far as his ingenuity will allow him. Man may unlock secret after secret in chemistry, in biology, in nuclear physics, in geology, in astronomy by the rigorous application of the scientific method. The natural realm is vast and man is free to search it to the utmost. But beyond it he cannot go by scientific method. Man's senses reach an end of what they can discover when they reach the end of the physical creation.

Some people assert that God does not exist because He cannot be observed by man. Some scientists and some university professors are especially prone to this point of view. Their eminence in one realm tends to blind men to their incompetence in another.

When a scientist, however brilliant and accomplished in his field, steps out of it and seeks to use the authority obtained in his discipline as a warrant to make pronouncements in an entirely unrelated area, it is an act of sheer arrogance. He leaves the bank in which he has huge deposits and walks into another, in which he has none, and swaggers as importantly there as in the place where his capital is. He is entitled to be hustled out as a pauper.

This is particularly so with regard to any attempt to apply credentials earned in the natural realm to the spiritual and supernatural realm. We know it is possible for a man to be an intellectual genius and a moral idiot; it is equally possible for a man of the highest attainment in the arts, letters, or science to be entirely ignorant regarding the spiritual and supernatural.

The natural man, whatever his gifts, remains fixedly inexpert in comprehending that which is beyond the physical creation. He may posit anything he wishes, but he cannot prove any of it.

My concern is not with what may be thought to be or with what may be imagined to be, but only with what may be *known* to be.

He Comes as Wind

Since nothing beyond the vast physical creation, consisting of matter and energy and all their interactions and relations, can be *scientifically* shown to exist, we must seek another method of proof.

The natural man is limited to the natural realm, where he has his existence. But that which has its existence in the spiritual realm is not limited to the spiritual realm. It may enter into the natural realm and do so with very pronounced effects upon it.

An enemy of Israel once sent "horses and chariots and a large army" by night to surround and seize the prophet Elisha. When Elisha's servant saw this, he ran and said, "Alas, my master! What shall we do?" Elisha replied, "Fear not, for they that are with us are more than they that are with them."

That seemed an odd declaration, because *no* soldiers were with Elisha. But Elisha prayed and said, "Lord, I pray thee, *open his eyes that he may see*." So the Lord "opened the eyes of the young man, and he saw, and behold the mountain was full of horses and chariots of fire round about Elisha." The young man who at first had seen only the army of Syria saw another army camped in that place, the army of the Lord. (2 Kings 6:14-17)

What he saw was not a vision but reality. He saw real horses and real chariots on the mountain, but they existed on a different plane of reality than the one on which man dwells. They could come into the natural order and affect it, but they were not a part of the natural order. They exist in an order beyond or above the natural, called the supernatural.

In this account—and at many other points in the Bible—the Scriptures tell of forces and events in the physical and natural realm and of forces and concurrent events in the spiritual and supernatural realm, both having a bearing on the outcome of history.

The chariots and the horsemen of Israel that Elisha's servant was permitted to see were supernatural and normally unseen, but they had taken their stations in the natural order and they were there to take effective action to protect the prophet Elisha and the nation Israel (see 2 Kings 6).

There are spiritual forces at work today causing changes of astonishing magnitude in human affairs. If we fail to recognize them we shall continue to be utterly helpless in dealing with their effects.

That there is a God is entirely outside of the capacity of science and the physical senses to discover by any method whatever. God is not found in the realm of the natural but He is found in the realm of the spiritual.

If that were the last word on the matter, we would be blind and unknowing forever. But it is not the last word. The Bible says:

Eye has not seen, nor *ear* heard, neither have entered into the heart of man, the things which God has prepared for them that love him. But *God has revealed them to us by His Spirit,* for the Spirit searches all things, yea, the deep things of God.

. . . The things of God *no man knows,* but the Spirit of God" knows them and reveals them to man (1 Corinthians 2:9-11).

There it is. If man is to know anything at all about the realm of the spiritual and the supernatural, it must be given to him by revelation. Revelation is a one-way avenue. It comes from the spiritual plane to the natural plane. It never runs the other way.

Until the young man's eyes were opened by God, in response to the prayer of Elisha, he saw nothing, knew nothing, suspected nothing of the chariots and the horsemen of Israel that were camped in that place.

The initiative in scientific discovery lies wholly with man. The initiative in spiritual revelation lies wholly with God. Men can know only what God elects to reveal to them about the spiritual and the supernatural.

If we are truthful, we are obliged to admit that we can know nothing whatever of life after death apart from revelation. We can know nothing whatever about heaven or hell apart from revelation. We can know nothing about angels or demons apart from revelation.

God has chosen to make an extensive revelation to man regarding these things. He has chosen to do so in a way that makes them readily intelligible to human beings.

There is a line of communication from the supernatural into the natural order. The personal agent of this communication is the Spirit of God, the Holy Spirit.

The Holy Spirit—He is a living Person—dwells in the spiritual order and He enters the natural order unseen. There are absolutely no limits on where He may go. In the Bible He is likened, in His comings and goings, to the wind: "The wind blows where it wishes and you hear the sound of it, but do not know where it comes from and where it is going" (John 3:8, NAS). Unseen the Holy Spirit comes; unseen He goes, yet there are effects of His wonderful presence among men.

The Holy Spirit takes of the truths of God, and of the spiritual realm, and conveys them according to the will of God, to men. In this He uses words primarily but occasionally also visions (pictures) and dreams as means of communication, so that what is revealed is made plainly intelligible to man.

Prophecy is an aspect of this revelation. True prophecy comes from God. Prophecy comes initially in the form of the spoken word through the lips of a prophet. It is imparted to a man or a woman by the Holy Spirit, and then, as the prophet speaks it out, men hear it and receive the prophecy.

Prophecy does not come because man wills it, but because God gives it.

Speaking of the Hebrew prophets, the New Testament says, "But know this first of all, that no prophecy of Scripture is a matter of one's own interpretation, for no prophecy was ever made by an act of human will, but men moved by the Holy Spirit spoke from God" (2 Peter 1:20, 21, NAS).

The prophets of Israel did not speak their own minds. Each spoke publicly that which the Holy Spirit imparted to him from God.

The prophet Joel, speaking the word of the Lord, declared: "I will pour out My Spirit on all flesh; and your sons and your daughters shall *prophesy,* your old men shall dream *dreams,* your young men shall see *visions*" (Joel 2:28). So the direct result of the coming of the Holy Spirit upon men and women is sometimes seen in inspired prophecies, dreams, and visions.

Testing Prophets and Dreamers of Dreams

Though they are the means God uses to convey His revelations to men, prophecy, dreams, or visions do not in themselves have any claim whatever to expressing truth. More false prophecy is uttered in the world than true prophecy, and by no close margin. Dreams flicker through our sleep like surrealist films in montage. Visions may, and often do, come from mental derangement or from evil spirits. It is only when the Holy Spirit uses these means that the content of the prophecy, the dream, or the vision is truth.

It is important to understand that factual accuracy does not constitute evidence that a prophecy or a dream or a vision is from God. Factual accuracy is not an adequate test of the divine inspiration of any prophecy.

The law of Moses speaks this word regarding prophecy: "If a prophet or a dreamer of dreams arises among you and gives you a sign or a wonder, and the sign or the wonder *comes true,* concerning which he spoke to you, saying, 'Let us go after other gods (whom you have not known)' . . . *you shall not listen to the words of that prophet* or that dreamer of dreams; for the Lord your God is testing you to find out if you love the Lord your God with all your heart and with all your soul. . . . But that prophet or that dreamer of dreams shall be put to death" (Deuteronomy 13:1-5, NAS).

True prophecy is, of course, always factually accurate, but that is not the acid test. The acid test of all prophecy is whether it is in or out of accord with the Scriptures. A prophecy may be factually accurate and spiritually wrong. In that case it is a counterfeit of divinely inspired prophecy designed to impress men intellectually but deceive them spiritually.

A prophecy can be supernatural, factually accurate and false! It is very likely that such a prophecy is factually accurate *because* it is supernatural. But it does not proceed from God, and the man or woman who speaks it is not a man or woman of God.

There are many false prophets and there is much false prophecy circulating in the United States today. False prophets have been coming very prominently to the fore in recent years. We can accurately define a false prophet as an individual who is spiritually connected to the supernatural, who speaks at times under the influence of supernatural powers, but whose authority as a prophet does not proceed from God and whose words and counsel are not in accord with the Word of God. In God's eyes, such a person is a great offender, because he deals in the supernatural—but not by God's commission!—and he dispenses spiritual counsel—in contradiction to God's Word!

Among the leading false prophets, by the terms of this biblical definition, whose statements are widely known in the United States today are:

The late Bishop James A. Pike. His experiments with the supernatural were in the most direct and explicit contradiction to the Word of God.

Jeane Dixon. She has supernatural powers that do not proceed from God. Some of her prophecies may be factually accurate—some clearly are, most are dead wrong—but she uses means that take a person into the supernatural by agents other than the Spirit of God.

Timothy Leary. He is under the strong influence

of supernatural powers. He is the person perhaps
most responsible for the introduction into America
of spiritual practices contrary to the Holy Scriptures.

There are many others. Some of them meet and
pass the test of factual accuracy at times. That does
not make them less false, it only makes them more
dangerous and more deceptive to the uninformed.

A false prophet must be distinguished from a
phony prophet. A false prophet has certain supernatural powers and uses them. A phony prophet is an
outright fake. A false prophet may be utterly sincere and unaware of his falsity. A phony prophet
knows he is a fake. A false prophet may practice
gross spiritual deception without knowing it, because he himself is thoroughly deceived. A phony
prophet knows exactly the deceptions he practices
and how he practices them.

Such people are still around and they still deceive
the ignorant, but we are mainly troubled now by
quite a different breed. Bishop Pike was not a fake.
He surely believed in what he was doing and in
what he was saying. He cannot be faulted on the
grounds of objective sincerity. He was deceived.

It is a singularly interesting and significant fact
that when supernatural gifts of the Holy Spirit that
are specifically described and approved in the Bible
began occurring in churches in his Episcopal diocese
in California, Bishop Pike argued against them and
sought to impede their exercise. Then he became
engaged in promulgating in our culture by the considerable means at his disposal supernatural practices that the Bible specifically identifies as contrary
to the will of God because they are harmful to man.

It has been widely reported that a minister, the
Rev. Arthur Ford, who was a very prominent medium, held the séance in which Bishop Pike received

messages from what he took to be his dead son.

The term medium is a very apt one. One definition is: "A person serving as an instrument through which another personality or a supernatural agency is alleged to manifest itself." The Bible clearly and repeatedly warns worshipers of God to have nothing to do with mediums at any time.

Many mediums who conduct séances are outright fakes. It is extremely unlikely that Mr. Ford was a fake. There is every reason to believe that he was, in fact, a medium.

At this point we must ask, a medium *from* what *to* what? Mr. Ford would claim to be a medium between dead human beings and living human beings. When he conducted the séance for Bishop Pike, he apparently succeeded in accurately speaking certain facts about the dead son to Bishop Pike, facts about which Mr. Ford probably had no prior knowledge. That is, he brought forth words and statements of factual accuracy by using supernatural powers. It is yet more precise to say that the medium Mr. Ford brought forth certain words by *being used* by certain supernatural powers. His spiritual accessibility to these powers is what made him a medium.

I do not dispute that a spirit took hold of Mr. Ford during this séance. I do not dispute in any way the likelihood that what Mr. Ford said was spoken under the immediate influence of supernatural powers. But the terrible fact is that the spirit that takes hold of a medium is not the spirit of a deceased human being but an evil, demonic spirit. The voice that speaks through the vocal organs of a medium in a séance is not the voice of a dead human being. It is the voice of an evil spirit impersonating the dead human being.

A medium who is not a fake, who is sincere in his

practice and in his adventures in the supernatural, brings men and women into direct contact with evil spirits. These evil spirits are engaged in active opposition to the will of God because they are the enemies of God. Their purpose is to draw human beings away from the truths of God, which set men free, and get them involved in practices against their well-being.

God wants man to know of, and to experience, that which is supernatural, but never that aspect of the supernatural which is Satanic.

It is as though a table were spread with mushrooms, half of them tender, succulent and fully edible, half of them deadly, all looking pretty much alike. Your friend will tell you which are which. He will say, "Eat all you can of that, and keep away from all of that."

Your enemy, who wants you to be destroyed, will say, "Dig in! Eat anything that looks good and tastes good! If you listen to that narrow-minded maker of distinctions you'll starve. Your friend doesn't want you to have any mushrooms." But the truth is he does. Your friend just doesn't want you to get any that will kill you.

In the supernatural realm there are two major spiritual forces. There is *the Holy Spirit*. And there are *evil spirits*. Everything supernatural which proceeds from the latter is dangerous to man and can be deadly.

The Scriptures of the Old and New Testaments constitute a full and reliable declaration of what is true on the spiritual plane. A Christian need never be "at sea" concerning God's will or about what is right or wrong, true or false, helpful or harmful. Jesus promised, "When He, the Spirit of truth, comes, He will guide you into all truth" (John 16:13a, NAS).

A Lady Named Lowe

A wonderful instance of God's effective communication to man by the Holy Spirit occurred in a church at Birmingham, England, several years ago. A friend and associate of mine, Mrs. Hannah Lowe, a missionary of more than 30 years standing to Bogota, Colombia, had spent some months working with orphans at Bethlehem, Jordan. On her way back to South America she stopped in England.

In London she met some Pentecostal people and it was suggested that she speak in several churches while in England, spending two nights in each church. Pentecostal churches frequently meet two or more nights in the week.

On a very cold night in late autumn Mrs. Lowe arrived to speak in the Birmingham church. The people were scattered about the church auditorium and she asked if they would move in closer to the pulpit. They would be more comfortable that way and she would not have to raise her voice to reach the last row of the pews. Nearly everyone moved, but one woman sat in an end seat in the last row, next to a radiator, and did not budge. Mrs. Lowe surmised that she felt extra cold and did not want to give up her place by the radiator.

Mrs. Lowe told of her missionary work in Colombia. As she finished, a vision flashed onto her consciousness. It was a picture—as vivid as a color slide —of an elephant with a bell standing in the thick green growth of a jungle.

Then the picture of the elephant was gone, and a second picture took its place. Mrs. Lowe saw milestones set at the side of a woodland road.

In a moment a third picture succeeded it. The experience was very much like a succession of photographic slides in brilliant focus. This third picture was of an hourglass. The yellow sand had almost all sifted through to the bottom half.

A fourth picture flashed on. It was a beautiful picture of a lonely beach in wintertime, a frosty scene at the edge of the sea. The sun shone overhead, but it looked small and feeble to impart much warmth. The waves were crashing in and as tongues of the sea licked the rocks, they almost caught and froze there. A thin film of ice clung to the rocks, but the sun was just strong enough to keep the water from forming solid ice.

As Mrs. Lowe wondered what to make of the visions, the four pictures were presented again, very rapidly, one by one in the same order, and they were as exact in their detail and as vivid as at the first: The elephant in the jungle with the bell. The milestones strung along the roadside. The hourglass with the sand almost run out. The beach, and the waves that were not quite freezing as they washed over the rocks.

Mrs. Lowe did not know in her mind what to do, but she opened her mouth and heard herself say these words:

"There is someone here tonight who has a call to India."

It was clear now that the elephant in the jungle signified India.

There was a momentary pause and Mrs. Lowe spoke again. *"You're not young anymore,"* she said. The words interpreted the vision of the milestones along the road, the passing of years. ("It was as if the Lord pieced it all together for me," Mrs. Lowe explained.)

"Time is running out for you," she said. *"You do not have much longer to decide."* These words matched the picture of the sand running out in the hourglass.

"Already your heart is becoming icy. A little longer and it will freeze entirely, but there is still a little warmth and it has not frozen yet. The sun of righteousness, God's Son, has warmed your heart even though that has seemed weak to you and He has kept your heart up until this time. Much time has passed. Now there is only a little time left, and He calls you to India."

"Is there anyone here who answers to this description?" she asked. "Will you come to the altar?"

At this invitation, the woman seated at the rear of the hall, apart from the rest of the congregation, got up, came quickly down the side aisle and dropped to her knees at the altar railing, praying and weeping.

After the service, the minister and his wife told Mrs. Lowe the woman's story. She was in her thirties. She had been born in India, and her parents had brought her home to England and to Birmingham when she was a child.

Eight years prior to that memorable evening, the woman had received what she believed to be the call of God to go to India as a missionary.

A missionary to India had passed through the church, had spoken eloquently, and the young woman had gone forward to the altar railing as a way of declaring that she desired to go as a missionary to India. The church stood behind her in the decision and money was supplied for her passage and for clothing and equipment.

She packed her belongings, bade her farewells, and traveled into Europe with the lady missionary to India. But something went wrong, there was some misunderstanding, and the missionary left her in Europe and went on alone. The young woman, uncertain about what to do next, got in touch with the church and was told to come back.

Almost immediately members of the church were torn between two opinions. Some said the woman's call to India was genuine but that an unfortunate circumstance had barred her way. Others said no. The call was not genuine. It had been a false emotional surge and the proof of that was that it had come to nothing. She should never have gone. These opinions solidified into factions that deeply split the church.

The young woman did not know the answer herself. Caught between two strong and contrary opinions, she did not know how to act. But she knew that her own case was portrayed with great precision in the words Mrs. Lowe spoke. Those sentences were a marvelously supernatural confirmation of her original call to India.

The church members who had judged the case wrongly—regarding the circumstance of an impediment to the woman's journey to India as plausible evidence of a divine veto—now saw their error, and the division in the church over the matter was thoroughly healed. So it was that a few words spoken, not by human knowledge or insight but in a wisdom imparted by the Holy Spirit, resolved a severe perplexity that had vexed the church for eight years. The pictures and the words cut like a sharp sword through a knot that could not be untied. The more church members had pulled on that knot the tighter it had become.

Mrs. Lowe returned to Colombia. One morning a long letter came from India. "Here I am," the letter began. "After you left, the people in the church sacrificed and did everything they could to get me the passage on the boat."

It is a wonderfully refreshing thing to attend church services where something real happens—where there is spiritual reality. When a prophet, or a prophetess, speaks by the momentary inspiration of the Holy Spirit the words may come like lightning or like dew, but they are always fresh and arresting and right to the point of immediate need.

In their profound distrust of the supernatural, in their militant avoidance of it, and in their insistence on stale rote, many houses of worship have won a reputation among young people as the dullest places in town. Instead of obtaining their knowledge of the supernatural from Scripture, young people are obtaining it where they can get it, and most of what they are getting now are the deadly counterfeits of Satan.

God, Who does not want young feet to be taken in snares, has given an accurate chart to the channels of the supernatural in the Bible, with areas of danger clearly marked. God is a good Father, and He wants us to have what is good and to avoid what is evil in the supernatural.

"Now suppose one of you fathers is asked by his son for a fish; he will not give him a snake instead of a fish, will he? Or if he is asked for an egg, he will not give him a scorpion, will he?" the Bible asks. "If you then, being evil, know how to give good gifts to your children, how much more shall your Heavenly Father give the Holy Spirit to those who ask Him?" (Luke 11:11-13, NAS)

Chapter 4

The Invisible God:
"I AM"

The central declaration of the Scriptures is that God *is*.

The constant affirmation of the Scriptures is that God *acts*.

It has always been a wonder to me that some men can read the Bible right through and leave God out of it. That is a tremendous feat of intellectual excision. Everything is attributed to nature and man, nothing is attributed to God. The presupposition behind it is that there is no God. It requires a deliberate and selective blindness that screens out much of what the Bible is about.

If a man reads the Bible that way, he fails completely to understand it.

The Bible is a book that pierces beyond the natural into the supernatural. A man who reduces it, by mental fiat, to the dead level of the natural, censors out of the Bible exactly what the book was given to make clear to man. He lays an edict upon his understanding not to grasp what the Bible is about.

The Bible asserts, uniformly and from the beginning to end, that there are different levels of intelligent and active life: beasts, man, angels, demons, Satan, God. More are unseen than are seen. All but the beasts are intelligent agents whose actions profoundly affect human history. To smash them all down to a single level of existence is to read the Bible with resolute unintelligence.

The intelligent way to read the Bible is not to lump everything together without discrimination, assigning to man or to nature the acts of God. The intelligent and discriminate way to read the Bible is to assign the acts of man to man, the acts of Satan to Satan, the acts of God to God, the acts of angels to angels, and the acts of demons to demons. To do that illuminates events. Not to do so obscures their causes. There are events today that are not intelligible apart from the biblical structure of reality.

The central declaration of the Scriptures is that God is. When God commissioned Moses to lead the people of Israel, Moses wondered if the people would accept his commission as genuinely divine. God said to Moses, "Thus you shall say to the sons of Israel: 'I AM has sent me to you'" (Exodus 3:14, NAS).

Through Isaiah God said, "For I am God, and there is no other; I am God, and there is no one like Me, declaring the end from the beginning and from ancient times things which have not been done" (Isaiah 46:9, 10a NAS).

The God of the Scriptures is a God of intelligent and purposeful and efficient activity. He is a God who acts—who acts in human history. He is a God who speaks, and the signature of His divinity is that what He speaks far in advance is fully acted out in history.

In Genesis, and throughout the Bible, we see God exercising attributes of volition and intelligence and personality and speech of which man is capable on a diminished scale, because man is made in the image of God.

There are scholars who scoff at this as "an anthropomorphic God." They fail to grasp that God deliberately speaks to man about Himself in terms understandable to man. When the infinite God speaks to finite man, He speaks in terms measured to the mind and experience of man, just as a parent in speaking to a child brings his words and illustrations within the range of a child's comprehension.

Genesis declares that "God said, 'Let Us make man in Our image, after Our likeness, and let them rule. . . .' And God created man in His image, in the image of God He created him; male and female, He created them. And God blessed them" (Genesis 1:26-28, NAS). God endowed the first man Adam with attributes of will and intelligence and speech, so that man was like his Creator.

Man was made in the image of God, but sin entered the human race and marred the image of God. Psalm 82:6, 7 says, "*You are gods, . . . children of the Most High, but you shall die like men . . .*"

The Invisible God

The Bible says that "God is a spirit" (John 4:24). He is invisible and He is immortal.

The invisible God has expressed Himself in the physical creation. His creative hand is seen in the natural order, but He does not dwell on that plane. "Since the creation of the world His invisible attributes, His eternal power and divine nature have been clearly seen, being understood through what has been made" (Romans 1:20, NAS).

God is a spirit, invisible to the eye of man, and He dwells on the spiritual plane. He is supernatural—that is, above nature. All that we see in the natural realm, from the intricate design of the atom to the great balanced wheels of the stars and galaxies, is the product of God's creative genius and His infinite power. Nature is His handiwork.

No one has ever seen God, the Bible says in John 1:18. He cannot be discovered in any way other than by His own self-revelation made to man at times and by the means of His own choosing.

God chose the Hebrew people to be the recipients and heralds of His revelation of Himself to mankind, and it is with the patriarchs that this unfolding revelation of God began.

God commenced His public revelation of Himself with Abraham and continued and expanded it through Isaac, Jacob, Joseph, Moses, David, and the Hebrew prophets.

A man may learn something *about* God through teaching, but he only comes to *know* God by a direct, personal revelation to himself. Jacob had learned about God and about the acts of God from his Hebrew fathers, but he did not know God until God revealed Himself to him.

Jacob made a journey to his uncle's house. Chapter 28 of Genesis says: "And he came to a certain place and spent the night there, because the sun had set; and he took one of the stones of the place and put it under his head, and lay down in that place. And he had a dream, and behold, a ladder was set on the earth with its top reaching to heaven. . . ." The Lord appeared personally to Jacob that night and spoke certain promises to him.

"Then Jacob awoke from his sleep and said, 'Surely the Lord is in this place, and *I did not know it.*' And he was afraid and said, 'How awesome is this place! This is none other than the house of God, and this is the gate of heaven.' " He named the place Bethel, "the house of God." (Story quoted from NAS).

It was, by all appearances, just an ordinary place when Jacob stopped there to rest. The setting did not impress him. He took a stone for his pillow and went off to sleep. Bethel was different only because God chose at that place, on that night, to reveal Himself to Jacob.

Then that place seemed "awesome . . . the house of God . . . the gate of heaven" (Genesis 28:17, NAS).

The God of the Hebrews is the only true God. He is a living being, supreme above all others in the universe, Creator of all that is, the Author of life.

The Scriptures speak of God:

—as "the invisible God" in Colossians 1:15.

—as "the King eternal, immortal, invisible, the only wise God" in 1 Timothy 1:17.

—as "Him who is invisible" in Hebrews 11:27.

This passage in Hebrews says that, "By faith [Moses left] Egypt, not fearing the wrath of the king [Pharaoh]; for he endured as *seeing Him who is invisible.*"

"God is the blessed and only Sovereign, the King of kings and Lord of lords, who alone possesses immortality and *dwells in unapproachable light,* whom *no man has seen or can see*" (1 Timothy 6:15, 16, NAS).

Psalm 104 says that God covers Himself "with light as with a garment."

The Scriptures admonish men, "Let us offer to God an acceptable service with reverence and awe; for *our God is a consuming fire*" (Hebrews 12:28b, 29, NAS).

"God is light and in Him there is no darkness at all," the Bible says in 1 John 1:5b. It says also that "the fear of the Lord is the beginning of wisdom" (Proverbs 9:10).

The Personal God

The God revealed by the Bible is a *personal*

God, who reveals Himself to individual men. He deals directly and personally with men. The prophet Hanani told Asa king of Judah, "The eyes of the Lord run to and fro throughout the whole earth, to show Himself strong in the behalf of them whose heart is perfect toward Him" (2 Chronicles 16:9).

Adam, when he had sinned, tried to hide from God in Eden, but God found him there. Men, in their sin, seek to hide themselves morally from God. Some say that there is no God, and that gives them a temporary and delusive relief from concern over the consequences of their sins. Others tell themselves that God is very remote and unconcerned with man; that God set the universe in motion and then went off to some distant eyrie in the heavens to attend to matters far more important than the affairs of men. Some say that "God is dead." Scholars especially are prone to regard it as vanity that God would take any particular notice of men. Their supposition is that the God of the cosmos could not be a God interested in fine details. All of these are ways of declaring that man is free to sin and go his own way because God is blind to sin or so withdrawn from humanity as to be indifferent to individual acts.

The Bible gives the flattest possible contradiction to this. It states that "even the very hairs of your head are all numbered" (Luke 12:7). The God who knows the number of the hairs of your head knows the number of the sins of your heart.

And the God who knows the number of your hairs also knows the number of the stars. "He counts the number of the stars; He gives names to all of them" (Psalm 147:4, NAS). Or, as Isaiah puts it in majestic poetry: "To whom then will you liken Me that I should be his equal? says the Holy One. Lift up your eyes on high and see who has created these stars, the One who leads forth their host by number; He calls them all by name. . . .

"Why do you say, O Jacob, and assert, O Israel, 'My way is hidden from the Lord and the justice due me escapes the notice of my God'?" (Isaiah 40:27, NAS).

Only lately, by probing outward from the earth with telescopes, has man begun to know something of the vastness of creation. The Milky Way alone is a system of over a hundred billion stars. It is just one galaxy. Other galaxies move in clusters and more than 1,000 of these have been found—1,000 clusters of galaxies.

"The galaxies within reach of telescopes like that on Mount Palomar probably number in the billions," it was reported in 1963. The atlas of the universe maps the sky out to a depth in space of 600 million light-years. (A light-year is about six trillion miles.) Isaac Asimov wrote in 1960 that "the 200-inch telescope can make out objects up to an estimated two billion light-years away, and there is no sign of an end of the universe—yet."

The galaxies *within reach* appear to number in the billions. If each galaxy is a family of billions of stars, we begin to get a notion of the extent of it— billions of billions—yet God knows the number of the stars and He "calls them all by their names."

The God of creation is the God of the cosmos to be sure. He is also the God of minute details.

Man has devised microscopes and particle accelerators that enable him to look inward upon the creation, and by them he has sliced matter down to fractions so fine as to make a billionth of an inch sound like an exceedingly crude measurement, but he has not yet managed to pierce to that which is so fine that it does not have clear structure and intelligent design.

An uncle of mine, Dr. Robert H. Phillips, is a nuclear physicist who worked for a dozen years at the Brookhaven National Laboratory on Long Island. He has occasionally given me an evening-long talk on the subatomic world (remember when we used to think of an atom as something terribly small?) and has told me of the precision of nuclear measurement.

Nuclear measurements carried out with a particle accelerator deal in "such sizes as 10 to the minus 25th square centimeters," he told me. "That means that if you put one over one and add twenty-five zeroes—

$$\frac{1}{10,000,000,000,000,000,000,000,000}$$

—then you have written the fraction of a square centimeter that a nucleon occupies in space." That is *one ten-septillionth of a square centimeter*.

"That isn't the very smallest thing that we look in on by any means," he said. "The subdivision of matter certainly reaches to smaller objects than that."

Nucleons are protons or neutrons. "Nobody really believes that a nucleon is the last subdivision of matter," Dr. Phillips said. Some physicists hypothesize quarks as still more elementary particles.

If man looks outward he sees the creative hand of God and he cannot search to the end of it, and if man looks inward he sees the creative hand of God and he has not yet come to the end of it.

Study everything between quarks and quasars and you find structure, motion, order, a lawful stability, arrangement, and design.

Whenever man seems to be near the inner or outer limits of the creation another layer unfolds to his astonished gaze. The God who made the planets also designed the molecule. He who formed man also formed the living cells. The God of the whole is also the God of the parts. And He cares particularly for man.

"Before him no creature is hidden, but all things are naked and laid bare to the eyes of him with whom we have to do" (Hebrews 4:13).

At a time of great decline of faith, even the elders of Israel said, "The Lord sees us not; the Lord has forsaken the earth" (Ezekiel 8:12).

Such things as that are said today by seminary professors training young men to be ministers. These statements were contrary to the fact then, and were evidence of the elders' wickedness and blindness, and they are just as false today.

The Bible declares, "Thou God seest me" (Genesis 16:13).

"Woe to those who deeply hide their plans from the Lord, and whose deeds are done in a dark place; and they say, 'Who sees us?' or 'Who knows us?' You turn things around! Shall the potter be considered as equal with the clay, that what is made should say to its maker, 'He did not make me'; or what is formed say to him who formed it, 'He has no understanding'?" (Isaiah 29:15, 16, NAS).

"O Lord, Thou hast searched me and known me!" David says. "Thou knowest when I sit down and when I rise up. Thou discernest my thoughts from afar. Thou searchest out my path and my lying down, and art acquainted with all my ways. Even before a word is on my tongue, lo, O Lord, Thou knowest it altogether. Thou dost beset me behind and before, and layest Thy hand upon me. . . . Wither shall I go from Thy Spirit? Or whither shall I flee from Thy presence? . . .

"For Thou didst form my inward parts, Thou didst knit me together in my mother's womb. . . . Thou knowest me right well; my frame was not hidden from Thee, when I was being made in secret, intricately wrought in the depths of the earth. Thy eyes beheld my unformed substance. In Thy book were written, every one of them, the days that were formed for me, when as yet there was none of them. . . . When I awake I am still with Thee. . . . Search me, O God, and know my heart! Try me and know my thoughts! And see if there be any wicked way in me, and lead me in the way everlasting!" (Psalm 139)

The Invisible God Made Visible

There is no more awesome and wonderful fact than that God, the Creator, in making Himself known to man, has come to man as man. Of the several means of revelation God uses to make known the truth about Himself, the one that is chief above all is the incarnation: God coming into human society as man.

We are living on a visited planet. That is far more than a New Testament idea. That God Himself— the Creator—would come to Israel as a man is prophesied in the most explicit terms in the Old Testament. Isaiah 9:6 says, "For unto us a Child is born, unto us a Son is given; and the government shall be upon His shoulder, and His name shall be called Wonderful, Counselor, The mighty God, The everlasting Father, The Prince of Peace."

Think of that: A man born a Jew—nothing less than Emanuel—God with us.

God made His most complete revelation of Himself to man in a Jew named Jesus. Jesus perfectly showed forth the character of God in His person. He, alone among all men, had no part in sin from birth to death. The Bible says of Jesus: "He is *the image of the invisible God,* the first-born of all creation. For in Him all things were created, both in the heavens and on earth, visible and invisible, whether thrones or dominions or rulers or authorities—all things have been created through Him and for Him. . . . For it was the Father's good pleasure for all the fulness [of God] to dwell in Him, and through Him to reconcile all things to Himself, having made peace through the blood of His cross" (Colossians 1:15-19, NAS).

Jesus made the invisible God visible to man in His own person. He claimed, in absolute harmony with the Old Testament prophecies of the Messiah, to have lived before His birth at Bethlehem. Jesus said, "I came forth from the Father, and have come into the world; I am leaving the world again, and going to the Father" (John 16:28, NAS). "Before Abraham was, I am," Jesus said (John 8:58). In that, He declared Himself to be God.

The Old Testament is explicit on the humanity and the divinity of the Messiah. The New Testament, in the declarations of Jesus as well as those of the apostles and writers, is unequivocal on the divinity of Jesus. He is "the express image" of God the Father, as Hebrews says, and therefore Jesus said, "He who has seen Me has seen the Father" (John 14:9, NAS).

You can learn about God by reading the Bible, but God wants more than that for you. He wants you to know Him personally. God specifically offers to come into your life in so definite a way that you will know He has come in; you will know He is there, with you and in you. He wants to walk with you every step of the way through your life. That is your highest privilege as a human being. It doesn't make any difference who you are. "God is no respecter of persons" (Acts 10:34). The social and class distinctions of the world count nothing with God. If you sit on the lowest rung of public respect and dignity, ignored by nearly everybody, God will come into your life. If you occupy the highest station, God will come into your life. As much is true if you are an ordinary person. After He had risen from the grave, Jesus said, "Behold, I stand at the door and knock; if any man hears My voice and opens the door, *I will come in to him* and will sup with him and he with Me" (Revelation 3:20).

God's Love and His Fury

Most men have heard that "God is love." The passage that declares this says: "Every one who loves is born of God and knows God. The one who does not love does not know God, for God is love. By this the love of God was manifested in us, that God has sent His only begotten Son into the world so that we might live through Him. In this is love, not that we loved God, but that He loved us and sent His Son to be the propitiation for our sins. Beloved, if God so loved us, we also ought to love one another. No one has beheld God at any time; if we love one another, God abides in us, and His love is perfected in us" (1 John 4:7b-12, NAS).

God created the world and man, and everything else that He created, as the expression of His generosity and love. "God saw that everything he had made . . . was very good." God intends that His creation be joyously perfect. He intends order, harmony, peace, worship, love, and great joy to prevail unchallenged among intelligent beings.

The beauty, the symmetry, the order and perfection, the sheer loveliness of what God made was all designed to serve the best interests of man and to afford him scope for achievement and discovery, endless provisions, pleasure and joy. It has been terribly impaired by the introduction into its affairs of the active principles of sin and self-will, whose effect is to spread blight and ruin in many different forms over the landscape of God's creation. One such blight is racial hatred, which has caused so much anguish and bloodshed among mankind.

Contrary to a very common notion of it, the quality of God's love is not bland. The love of God is strong. The love of God is discriminate, and it is purposeful. The perfect complement to the love of God—that which throws it into strong relief and shows its purity—is the hatred that God expresses toward that which is evil. God hates sin. He hates evil.

The greater an individual's sensitivity to that which violates what he truly prizes, the less patience he has with it. A love of purity requires by its nature a coequal abhorrence of filth. A symphony orchestra conductor will not rest until he drives everything that mars the symmetry, beauty, and perfection of the music out of the performance. He is intolerant of that which disfigures it musically, and the greater his love of the score the more absolute his intolerance becomes.

Because He is love, God is consistently intolerant of everything that violates His own intention in creation. God hates evil with a pure and furious hatred because He sees that it is constantly at work to destroy what He has made—at work to destroy man, to destroy society, to destroy nature, to destroy civilization, to destroy harmony, to destroy joy. He does not look upon it as man does, that is, relatively, because He sees it not limitedly but in the whole path of its effective ruination.

The intention of Satan is to make moral, spiritual, and physical chaos and wreckage out of as much of

God's creation as he possibly can. Satan enlists man in that attempt, by appealing to his lawless lusts and passions. We can see the effects of that all around us, in the nation, in the world.

Man is infected with the moral disease that God calls sin. God is not tolerant of human sin because He knows that if it were allowed to go unarrested it would ultimately destroy everything in its reach.

God loves the man but He hates the sin. It is God's will to separate the man from the sin, but if a man refuses to be separated from his sin, if he exhibits a resolute preference for it, then he must bear the full penalty for it, death. God will put such a man in quarantine forever in a fire prepared for the devil. The Bible declares that sin must be arrested and judged.

God seeks to separate the sinner from the sin, so that He may express His pure love to the sinner and His pure wrath against the sin. That is what He did in sending Jesus to die on the cross for sin. God placed man's sin upon Jesus at Calvary and judged it there with the penalty of death. He bore "our sins in His own body on the tree" (1 Peter 2:24a). The love of God is strong. Strong enough to send His Son to die for sin.

God's love is expressed in the creation, but it is supremely expressed in the redemption. God cannot go farther in loving man and in dealing with sin than to die for sin.

The anger of God against evil is shown not less in the New Testament than in the Old. The New Testament is full of the expressed fury of God at evil, including the outpouring of God's wrath as depicted in the Book of The Revelation.

Jesus' love is seen in the Gospels, and so is His fury at sin and dissimulation. Matthew, chapter 23, records Jesus' address to the religious leaders: "Woe to you, hypocrites . . . blind guides . . . blind fools . . . hypocrites! . . . You serpents . . . vipers, how can you escape the damnation of hell?"

It is written of the Son of God, "You have *loved righteousness*, and *hated iniquity;* therefore God, thy God, has anointed you with the oil of gladness above your fellows" (Hebrews 1:9).

Jesus repeatedly warned men that if they continued in sin they would at last "be cast into hell, where their worm does not die, and the fire is not quenched." He counseled, "If your hand causes you to stumble, cut it off; it is better for you to enter life crippled, than having your two hands, to go into hell, into the unquenchable fire" (Mark 9:43, NAS). He said, "The Son of Man"—speaking of Himself—"will send forth His angels, and they will gather out of His kingdom all stumbling blocks, and those who commit lawlessness, and will cast them into the furnace of fire; in that place there shall be weeping and gnashing of teeth. Then the righteous will shine forth as the sun in the kingdom of their Father. He who has ears, let him hear" (Matthew 13:41-43, NAS).

When there is a fire, true love warns of the fire; love will not say there is no fire. God's love seeks to keep men from a destiny of fire.

God will not depart by so much as a shade from His original plan for a perfect and joyous creation. The judgment is a necessary stage in the fulfillment of His great purpose, but the purpose of His love does not end there. At judgment there will be a complete separation of the just from the unjust and a complete, eternal exclusion of the unjust from any participation in the future. When they are put away. God's program will go on.

Chapter 5

The Biblical Structure of Reality

The Bible declares that the God who revealed Himself to Israel is the Creator and Ruler of the universe.

It reveals that there is an order of intelligent created beings who are the servants of God, called angels.

The Bible reveals an order of intelligent beings who are in active rebellion against God, called evil spirits or demons.

The Bible declares that they are led by an intelligent personality called Satan.

These truths can be ignored, but they cannot be escaped. Saying that demons do not exist in no way prevents them from intruding into the lives and the affairs of your family.

We need to know about *reality*, spiritual reality as well as physical reality.

The rational man ought to agree that if God declares by revelation that there is a being called Satan, who actively and radically opposes all the purposes of God among men and who works with skill and inexhaustible energy against the best interests of men, it is a good thing for man to know it. In the biblical revelation, Satan is fully exposed as the enemy of God and man.

By the same token, Satan generally seeks desperately to conceal the fact of his existence. His meth-

ods depend, for their effectiveness, on the conceal-
ment both of their source and their purpose. Except
for those who would worship him forthrightly,
Satan does not want people to believe that he exists.
He wants you to believe positively that he does *not*
exist. Then he may go about his business against
you and against your family undetected and unsuspected.

Rational men, accustomed as they are to equating
the name of Satan with a variety of purely fantastic
caricatures, are a little too quick to smile knowingly
when his name is mentioned. One of Satan's devices
has been to promote ridiculous caricatures of himself that are so evidently not real that rational men
associate his name with the mythical. Because of
this, intelligent people have too readily come to
equate the name and person of Satan with a scheme
of thought that is fanciful, at best, and therefore intellectually contemptible.

The Bible is not talking about that kind of figure
at all. Satan bears about as much resemblance to
the figures in these myths as the God of the Hebrews
does to Santa Claus.

Angels

There is an intelligent order of created beings
who serve God, called angels. They have to do with
God and they also have to do with man. Angels are
in many ways much like men. They possess attributes of intellect, personality and will similar to
those of man. Angels can speak. So like men are the
angels that it is possible to sit and talk with one and
not to know that he is an angel. The New Testament says, "Be not forgetful to entertain strangers,
for thereby some have entertained angels un-
awares" (Hebrews 13:2).

Angels are spiritual beings. They dwell on the spiritual plane, above nature. They are normally invisible to man. They enter the natural order, visibly and invisibly, but it is not their primary abode. They stand a step higher on the ladder of creation than man.

Man, who is set at the summit of the natural order, was made "a little lower than the angels" in the scale of creation. David wrote, "When I consider Thy heavens, the work of Thy fingers, the moon and the stars, which Thou hast ordained, What is man, that Thou are mindful of him . . . ? For Thou hast made him a little lower than the angels, and hast crowned him with glory and honor" (Psalm 8:3-5).

The whole natural order, including man's physical body, is mortal. The angels are immortal. They are not subject to disease or death.

Angels can, at will, enter the natural realm. They can submit to and obey its laws; but they can, at will, leave it and ignore its laws and limitations. Far more significantly, angels can inhabit the natural realm without being observed and without being restricted by its laws. They move, unseen, among men, accomplishing their appointed work.

When angels visit men visibly, they come into the natural realm and often show themselves in the physical likeness of men. That which is invisible becomes visible, and the angels move among men as men.

In chapter 19 of Genesis we read that "two angels came to Sodom in the evening, and Lot was sitting in the gate." Lot arose and invited them to his house to "spend the night and wash your feet . . . and he made them a feast . . and they ate." They were angels, not men, yet they had feet to be washed and mouths with which to eat men's food. Psalms 78:25

says that, when God gave Israel manna to eat man ate *the bread of angels.*

The angels' purpose is to serve God and to carry out His orders. What angels do to and for a man is based entirely on the man's relationship to God. The angels protect and assist men who serve God. Sometimes they hinder and they destroy men. God has a plan in history and the angels have a role in advancing that plan.

I heard Dr. Charles E. Fuller, founder of Fuller Theological Seminary, tell of a highway accident in which the car he was driving went off the road and turned over. He said that, as the car turned over, he momentarily saw angelic protectors completely surrounding him, and he received not a scratch in an extremely dangerous accident. He said that, while he was turning upside down, he saw himself fully enveloped in light.

Psalm 104 says that God "makes His angels spirits; His ministers a flaming fire."

There are three key words there—"angels" . . . "spirits" . . . "ministers." Hebrews 1:14 affirms that the angels are "all ministering spirits," sent forth by God to minister to men. The word angel literally means messenger.

The angel Gabriel was sent to the prophet Daniel to explain a vision concerning future events. (Daniel 8:16, 17).

The same Gabriel appeared to the priest Zechariah and announced that he would have a son to be named John, the promised forerunner of the Lord Jesus Christ. The angel said, "I am Gabriel, who stands in the presence of God; and I have been sent to speak to you, and to bring you this good news" (Luke 1:19, NAS).

The birth of Jesus was announced by angels to shepherds in the fields. "And an angel of the Lord suddenly stood before them, and the glory of the Lord shone around them; and they were terribly frightened. And the angel said to them, 'Do not be afraid; for behold, I bring you good news of a great joy . . ." (Luke 2:9-10, NAS).

Once Jesus fasted for a very long time. At length it was over, "and, behold, angels came and ministered to Him" (Matthew 4:11).

The angels constitute a numerous company. "The chariots of God are twenty thousand, even thousands of angels; the Lord is among them, as in Sinai, in the holy place" (Psalm 68:17). Jesus said that, at His bidding, 12 legions (50,000 to 60,000) of angels would come from heaven. Hebrews 12:22 speaks of "the city of the living God, the heavenly Jerusalem, and an innumerable company of angels." John writes, "And I looked, and I heard the voice of many angels around the throne, . . . and the number of them was myriads of myriads, and thousands of thousands" (Revelation 5:11, NAS).

Daniel was once shut into a pit of lions for defying an edict against worshiping God, but he was not harmed. When the king came to find what had happened, Daniel said, "O king, live for ever! My God has sent his angel, and has shut the lions' mouths, and they have not hurt me . . ." (Daniel 6:21, 22).

Angels are extremely powerful, and their power can be applied with force in the physical realm. The Bible describes them as "mighty . . . who carry out His [God's] orders" (Psalm 103:20, LB) and says that angels are "greater in power and strength than men (2 Peter 2:11, LB).

Before the resurrection of Jesus, His body was put in a tomb cut out of rock. A large stone was placed against the door of the tomb. A guard of soldiers was sent to make the tomb secure. They sealed the stone and set a guard there. "And behold, there was a great earthquake, for the angel of the Lord descended from heaven, and came and rolled back the stone from the door, and sat upon it. His countenance was like lightning, and his raiment white as snow. And for fear of him the keepers [guards] trembled and became like dead men" (Matthew 28:2, 3).

Angels have the power to destroy. The two angels who visited Lot told him to get out of Sodom with his family in the morning, "for we will destroy this place . . . the Lord has sent us to destroy it" (Genesis 19:12, 13).

Angels are seen in the Scriptures executing the judgments of God. In the great judgments that are to fall upon the earth, as detailed in Revelation, chapters 8 and 9, God's angels are centrally involved.

The day is coming "when the Lord Jesus shall be revealed from heaven with His mighty angels, in flaming fire taking vengeance on those who know not God" (2 Thessalonians 1:7, 8). "So it will be at the end of the age; the angels shall come forth, and take out the wicked from among the righteous, and will cast them into the furnace of fire; there shall be weeping and gnashing of teeth," Jesus declared (Matthew 13:49, 50, NAS). "For the Lord Himself shall descend from heaven with a shout, with the voice of the archangel, and with the trumpet of God, and the dead in Christ shall rise first" (1 Thessalonians 4:16).

Jesus once told the multitude that was following Him, "Whoever, therefore, is ashamed of Me and My words in this adulterous and sinful generation, of him also will the Son of man be ashamed, when He comes in the glory of His Fathter with the holy angels" (Mark 8:38).

Satan

The Bible declares that God has an archenemy: Satan. He is man's archenemy, too. Satan is at work today in the world, and in the United States, with an intensity unmatched in our experience. The Scriptures warn that his activity will be stepped up greatly among the nations, both in degree and in velocity, in the years immediately ahead. Satan desires to organize mankind for its own destruction. Unless we know of him and how he works, we will be caught short and find ourselves unable to cope with the events that descend upon us. To a degree, such is already the case.

One of Satan's primary aims is the destruction of man, and he can work much more effectively to destroy you if you think he is not working at it.

We can know nothing about the true nature of Satan apart from the Scriptures. Only the Bible reveals him to the understanding of man, and we need desperately to know about him, because what Satan does, and how he does it, are the concealed, powerful factors behind present eruptions of evil in the world.

The Bible is very clear about Satan's origin and person, his purposes, his power, and his domain. It tells a great deal about him in the Old and the New Testaments. Satan is seen at work in Genesis, the first book of the Bible, and in Revelation, the last book, and he is seen at scores of places in between.

There are today many appeals to "tell it like it is," to rip off all the sham and the pretense, to lay matters bare to their roots. That is exactly what the Bible does. It tells it as it really is. It tears away the camouflage, the coverup, and exposes this architect of evil: who he is and how he works.

Satan's name means "adversary." He was at his

creation a very beautiful being. His beauty has been corrupted by evil, but he still disguises and presents himself to much of mankind as god. He can do so, because the Bible says that Satan is a god.

The Bible declares that "God is a spirit." It describes angels as "ministering spirits." The Bible calls Satan *the prince of the power of the air, the spirit that now worketh in the children of disobedience*" (Ephesians 2:2). Satan is a spirit—that is, an intelligent living being, invisible to the natural eye.

This one portion tells us a great deal: First, that Satan is a prince, a ruler. Second, that his domain is centered in the atmosphere of the earth. Third, that he is active, or "at work." Fourth, that his activity is carried out through the lives of fallen or sinful men, who are called "the children of disobedience." It is a stark fact that Satan exercises some degree of actual authority and control over all men who have never become worshipers of the one true God. God is not the spiritual leader of most men. Satan is. That is why the Bible calls him "the god of this world" (2 Corinthians 4:4).

The name Satan does not speak of an impersonal influence. It speaks of a single, identifiable, distinct living being with a will, a personality, and a highly directed intelligence.

Satan has succeeded in usurping the place that belongs to God among the masses of mankind. He has substituted his will for the will of the living God in the lives of millions of men. That is why there is so much hell on the earth. Satan has taken the central place that God ought to occupy in the lives of men and has filled it up with other things—including false religion.

Satan is a ruler, and he is consistently spoken of in terms of royal power. As well as being designated "the god of this world," he is called "the prince of this world" (John 12:31).

Like all other created beings, however, Satan can only be in one place at a time. He is not omnipresent, as God is, but he manages to seem ubiquitous. Because he exists on the spiritual plane, he is able to move with almost instantaneous speed in the universe.

"Resist the devil," the Bible says, "and he will flee from you" (James 4:7). You cannot resist him, of course, if you do not believe he is there.

The Author of Idolatry

Satan is a spiritual leader. As the head of the rebellion against God and against the government of God, he works, using every means he can, to see that God is supplanted as the center of man's desire.

He does not greatly care to what secondary object or desire or pursuit a man gives his chief loyalty, so long as it is not to God, the source of life and of truth. He works constantly to divert man's attention from God, to direct it to something else. It may be to money, property, fame, power, pleasure, the family, success, science, art, a religious idol, a dead saint, a human leader, a false god, a political system, or anything else. Whatever it is, other than God, that takes first place in a man's life is that man's idol, and Satan is the author of idolatry.

The thing that takes the place of God in a man's life is Satan's substitute for God. Find out to what a man's ultimate loyalty goes, and that is his god.

If there is anything a man wants more than God, that thing will bar the gates of heaven to him forever. He is an idolater. He has put the creation in the place of the Creator. He is absorbed with a thing, when he ought to be absorbed with a Person.

God delights to have men enjoy good things. But He abhors it when a man takes those things and makes them his gods, thereby working his own corruption. Matthew 6:32, 33, sums it up: "Your heavenly Father knows that you have need of all these things. But seek *first* the kingdom of God and His righteousness, and all these things shall be *added* unto you." It is when we seek them first, and they become our chief delight, that we are guilty of idolatry. In doing that we make ends out of what were meant to be means.

Satan lusts for worship. Because it belongs exclusively to God, Satan desires it for himself. He would rather have worship than anything else, but because he knows he would not succeed in getting great numbers of men to worship him—if they knew that that was what they were doing—he sets up many objects as alternatives to the worship of God.

God never intended, anywhere in all the universe, idols to be set up as religious objects. Moses spoke for God in commanding: "Turn not ye unto idols, nor make for yourself molten gods: I am the Lord your God" (Leviticus 19:4).

God warned the Jews through Moses, "I will destroy your high places, and cut down your images, and cast your own dead bodies upon the dead bodies of your idols, and my soul shall abhor you . . . And I will scatter you among the heathen, and will draw out a sword after you, and your land shall be desolate, and your cities waste . . . ; then shall the land rest and enjoy her sabbaths" (Leviticus 26:30-34).

So profound is the effect of religious idols and images upon a land that the land of Israel could not "rest and enjoy her sabbaths" while the people practiced idolatry in it. It was better in God's sight for the people to be taken away and the land emptied of its population than for it to continue to be defiled.

There are those who do not worship physical idols but who worship evil spirits, including the devil. There are in this nation those who now openly worship the devil, in such religions as Satanism.

Satan's Policy of Lies

Suppression and contradiction of the Word of God are the supreme means by which Satan opposes God among men. His policy is to suppress the Scriptures wherever he can—that is, wherever he can get men to cooperate with him in that purpose. There have been in the past, and there are today, nations in which the possession and reading of the Scriptures is forbidden or restricted by every means available. Such nations are carrying out the policy of Satan against the dissemination of the knowledge of God. Satan hates the Scriptures because they reveal God and because they expose him.

Where he cannot suppress the Scriptures, he contradicts them, distorts them, heaps scorn upon them, causes them to be misapplied, and seeks by every possible means to nullify or severely limit their actual influence. Satan has turned many universities, once centers for study and promulgation of the truths of the Scriptures, into centers where God's Word is mocked and repudiated, with guile, enmity, sophistication, and a false show of scholarly objectivity. Much contradiction of the Scriptures in classrooms is purely gratuitous—dragged in by the teacher with no relevance to anything but his own arrogant bias—and part of it is a matter of scruple by deceived men. The effect is, as it long has been in this country, profoundly to subvert the Bible's influence among young people, leaving them without defense against the undermining of their character and morals. Steal the influence of the Bible, once so great, away from the German youth and you have, at the end, a generation of storm troopers and goose-steppers—mobilized by Satan for great destruction. Steal the influence of the Bible, once so great, away from American young people and you have what we are now beginning to have, a generation of militant and articulate anarchists—also mobilizing under the influence of Satan for destruction.

God cannot lie. His word is truth. In contrast to this, the Bible says of Satan, "When he lies, he speaks according to his own nature, for *he is a liar and the father of lies*" (John 8:44b).

It is the nature of Satan to speak lies. He is a liar, but more than that, he is "the father of lies."

A lie is designed to deceive. Satan does not present his lies as lies, but as truth. Satan's lies are designed to deceive men about the most important things: about God and the nature of God; about sin and evil; about redemption and salvation; about death; about judgment and hell. Satan's lies are designed to deceive men until their death. He is the father of the religious lie, which contradicts the Word of God and betrays men's souls forever if they believe it. He is the father of the political lie, which, when men accept it, leads them to national enslavement or destruction.

It is Satan's policy to challenge the Word of God directly, and specifically to contradict it. Because God is active in promulgating truth and Satan is active in promoting lies, *every man stands between the truth of God and the lies of Satan, and he must decide which to believe.*

Satan began his policy of lies in Eden. God told man, "From any tree of the garden you may eat freely; but from the tree of the knowledge of good and evil you shall not eat, for in the day that you eat from it you shall surely die" (Genesis 2:16, 17, NAS). Satan told the woman, "You surely shall not die! For God knows that in the day you eat from it your eyes will be opened, and you will be like God, knowing good and evil" (Genesis 3:4, 5).

Satan's purpose was death for man. His method was flat contradiction of what God had said. He sought to make his lie more acceptable by adding a promise of knowledge to it. Satan often tries to sweeten his lies that way. His method is rather like that of the fisherman who baits the hook with something delightful and apparently much to be desired. That is his *offer* to the fish. But it is not his purpose. His purpose is death.

It is time for the young, especially, to refuse to believe his lies, which promise liberation and lead to enslavement.

God is the Creator. Satan is the destroyer.

God created everything that is. Satan has never created anything. He cannot create anything. But he has destroyed much. He desires to destroy as much of God's creation as he can. He seeks to enlist man in that pursuit.

Satan needs men. He could never have gained any influence in the earth apart from securing the willingness of men to obey him and to disobey God, to believe him and to doubt God. He could never have brought death to the garden if Eve had not agreed with him. Satan operates by gaining the consent of man—to lies, to sin, to every kind of evil.

Satan's unvarying practice is to attempt to make a league with something in the fallen nature of every man, and to use that to lead the man first to sin and ultimately to destruction. The thing on which he tries to seize is different in different individuals. It may not be something as sharp and interesting as greed. It may be something as dull as sloth.

I know a young man who showed a genuine interest in the truths of Scripture, but who could be counted upon to fail to meet every appointment, regardless of the hour, because he was either dead-tired or dead-asleep. This continued over a period of years. Once, I made an appointment to meet him at 6:30 P.M. for a banquet at which a minister was to speak. My friend did not show up. A call to his home roused him from sleep, but too late for the occasion.

I could have shouted Proverbs 6:9-11 at him through the phone: "How long will you sleep, O sluggard? When will you arise out of sleep? Yet a little sleep, a little slumber, a little folding of the hands to sleep. So shall thy poverty come as one that travelleth, and thy want like an armed man."

The power of resistance to Satan, for every individual and every society, lies in obedience to the truth and conscience. If they cast aside the truth and trample conscience, they leave themselves wide open to Satan's strategy for their destruction.

Satan is right now heavily engaged in the process of attempting to destroy American society. Satan's frontlash against this nation at the moment is a largely irrational, anarchistic, rebellious mutation of Marxism, tied to free-love morals and street disorders. His backlash is likely to be ironfisted fascistic repression. The nation is being ripened for the appearance of a shrewd and eloquent demagogue, a man skilled in the manipulation of people's fears and emotions as a means of obtaining power. Though the radical Left may rock and shake America, the chances of this frontlash taking over in the nation are extremely remote. The chances of the backlash coming into power on a wave of popular revulsion and fear are far greater. Until now, there have been great balances in American society. They have preserved us from extremisms of the Left and Right, but we do not know how much longer these balances will hold the nation to a middle course of liberty and law and effective reform by democratic processes.

God save this nation from the vile conflict in which the revolutionary Marxists offer to save us from the fascists, and the fascists vow to save us from the Marxists. The Czechoslovaks have been through that cycle since World War II, and they know that it is all darkness and gall.

Men live either in liberty or in tyranny. By far the majority of men in history have had tyranny for their portion. Satan wills tyranny for men. It is only as the truths of the Bible break the power of Satan over men that liberty comes to the people.

"Where the Spirit of the Lord is, there is liberty," the Scriptures say (2 Corinthians 3:17). God is the author of liberty, and He wills liberty for man. Where men honor God, worship Him, and hold His Word in respect, liberty flows to them.

American society was, from colonial days, a Bible-influenced society. The public standard in this country was, to a remarkable degree, a biblical standard for quite a long time. Among the early presidents of the nation were several who rarely let a day go by without spending time reading the Bible. The churches, by and large, upheld the Scriptures and proclaimed their truths.

The effective attack on the Bible as the public standard in the nation began late in the last century, and it gathered great momentum after World War I. The consequences have been piling up on the nation heavily in the last few years. Satan has been destroying the foundation of the society in order that he may destroy the society.

The public standard of morality in the nation—at least as it is reflected in literature, motion pictures, advertising, and the arts—is now beginning to approximate that of Sodom. Crime, drug addiction, violence, family instability, and social instability have all been steeply on the rise.

Liberty, order, justice, and conditions that allow human beings a maximum of freedom and happiness are extremely displeasing to Satan, who hates men only less than he hates God. In his adroit parody, "Screwtape Proposes a Toast," C. S. Lewis quotes a devil as saying, "It was a bitter blow to us—it still is—that any sort of men who had been hungry would be fed or any who had long worn chains should have them struck off." The United States has afforded liberty and abundance and safety to millions of men in proportions far above what had ever been known in the world. Satan's strategy for taking these things away has been the continual diminishing of the influence of the Scriptures among the people.

The Scriptures have both a restrictive and a liberating effect. Where they are honored, they restrict sin, misery, and evil and check religious and political tyranny. Men are thus made free to expand along lines that are most beneficial to them individually and to society.

The polarization of a free society between extremes is the beginning of its destruction.

For all their venomous antagonism, the extreme Left and the extreme Right are not really two separate programs for taking over and wrecking the nation. They are two parts of *one single mechanism* whose ultimate intention is tyranny and whose chief manipulator is the devil.

The two extremes feed upon each other. The extreme Right must have the extreme Left as its foil if it is to make headway with the public. Both train their real attack on things that stand between them and total power—the free press, the independent judiciary, the electoral process, the balance of powers in the government. The devil doesn't care whether he takes over the country with his left hand or his right hand.

Consider the allegory of the Scarecrow and the Soldiers. A certain man—John America—lives on a spacious and fruitful farm on which things have gone rather well for a very long time. Another man—J. Harry Diablos—is bitter about how well things have gone for John. He wants to wreck his place or at least bring it closer to the standard of human misery that has prevailed in much of the rest of the world. So he hires some yippies and a squad of soldiers. He sends the yippies over to the farm to set themselves up as squatters, to poach on the land, to strew garbage around and openly to violate most of the conventions of morality and civility John is used to. They are his scarecrow. When John is sufficiently scared by what he sees, the man brings the soldiers over.

"Look, John," he says, "those derelict yippies out there are a terrible threat to your place. They'll make a mess out of it. Now, see those smart-looking fellows out there, with the short haircuts and the shiny boots? They're my soldiers. Just look at them, and you know you can trust them. Let my soldiers come onto your place and clean them yippies out." Old John agrees. The soldiers come in and clean the yippies out, but then they take over the place.

Satan's tactic for the destruction of American liberty is the manipulation of evil forces in a way that will finally cause the people to act rashly in alarm, rather than wisely in justice.

He has set the yippies up to give ordinary Americans a bad case of cultural shock, bafflement, and fear—yielding eventually perhaps to dumb fury.

A fascist or Marxist extremist could not gain a majority of the American vote if either presented himself in just that color. But in taking over, extremism seeks some issue, some single issue, to which a majority of the electorate *will* respond. It seizes that issue and rides it into power.

All extremism wants is for the people *legally to grant it a share of real power*. It will put on almost any face to get them to do that. Once it gets its grip on the jugular centers of national life and power, it will not stop until it has strangled liberty. You can vote them in, but you can never vote them out.

Satan is a dealer in sin. He tempts men and women, teen-agers, children, to sin because it suits his purposes to do so. Your sin, whatever it is, is Satan's claim upon you. He wants to hold that claim and, in time, to expand it.

A man in sin devotes some or all of his faculties, his time, his energy, his money, and his bodily members to works of sin. Whether he does so to greater or lesser measure, he has consecrated himself to that extent to Satan's rebellion against God. The Apostle John writes, "He who commits sin is of the devil" (1 John 3:8a).

Sin has a personal effect, a family effect, and a social effect. The influence of one man's sin can, at its apex, reach out to affect a nation or a series of nations. One man, Hitler, lent himself unreservedly to his hatreds and lusts, and because of that graves were dug all across the face of Europe. Out of one man's evil intentions, ultimately millions died.

Chapter 6

Battle for Allegiance

The earth we live on is the chief locale, the theater in the universe, of a challenge by Satan to the supremacy of God over a portion of His creation. Its inhabitants are the objects of what may accurately be called a contest between Satan and God for obedience and worship. This conflict is so severe that the Bible calls it "warfare," and men are very much at its center.

Satan hates that any men—that even one man—should worship God and love Him supremely. One of the desires of Satan is to show, if he can, that every man has his price, that no man loves God so well that he will allow nothing to stop him from worshiping and trusting Him. That is why God allowed a man named Job to stand a severe test of affliction. God knew that Job would not fail or fall.

Though the primary scene of Satan's activity is the earth and the atmosphere of the earth, Satan also has access to God (see Job 1:6-8, NAS): "Now there was a day when the sons of God came to present themselves before the Lord, Satan also came among them. And the Lord said to Satan, 'From where do you come?' Then Satan answered the Lord and said, 'From roaming about on the earth and walking around on it.'

"And the Lord said to Satan, 'Have you considered My servant Job? For there is no one like him on the earth, a blameless and upright man, fearing God and turning away from evil.' "

The reply of Satan affords a glimpse of his character. "Then Satan answered the Lord, 'Does Job fear God for nothing? Have You not made a hedge about him and his house and all that he has, on every side? You have blessed the work of his hands, and his possessions have increased in the land. But put forth Your hand now and touch all that he has; he will surely curse You to Your face.' " What a combination of cynicism, skepticism, accusation, and hatred breathes in that speech!

We are here shown a restriction that was upon the activity of Satan toward the man Job, a restriction that Satan found extremely frustrating. He could not get at Job because God had "made a hedge about him and his house and all that he has, on every side." It was an invisible barrier, set up by the decree of God, and Satan and his demons could not get past it.

Satan therefore accused Job of worshiping God for gain. He asked God to wipe Job out—"touch all that he has; he will surely curse You to Your face."

"And the Lord said to Satan, 'Behold, all that he has is in your power, only do not put forth your hand on him.' So Satan departed from the presence of the Lord" (Job 1:10-12, NAS).

Satan now had what he wanted, access to Job, and he was sure he could prove that Job was not a disinterested worshiper of God.

A series of calamities fell upon Job in a single day. These came by the direct activity of Satan, but it is interesting to see their immediate sources. From one side, a party of the Sabeans invaded his property. They stole his animals and slew the servants. From another side, the Chaldeans formed three companies and swept suddenly down upon Job's property in a devastating raid. Men in action, yes, *but Satan in action behind them!* At almost the same time, a fire broke out in the property and shortly thereafter "a great wind came from across the wilderness and struck the four corners of the house," and it collapsed, killing his sons and his daughters. Natural forces, yes, but Satan in action behind them!

"Then Job arose and tore his robe and shaved his head, and he fell to the ground and worshiped. And he said, 'Naked I came from my mother's womb, and naked I shall return there. The Lord gave and the Lord has taken away. Blessed be the name of the Lord' " (Job 1:20, 21, NAS).

His words gave the lie to Satan's accusation! Job stood in the test. God told Satan that Job had "held fast his integrity." But Satan, not easily defeated, was not satisfied.

"And Satan answered the Lord and said, 'Skin for skin! Yes, all that a man has he will give for his life. However, put forth Your hand, now, and touch his bone and his flesh; he will curse You to Your face.' So the Lord said to Satan, "Behold, he is in your power; only spare his life" (Job 2:4-6, NAS).

Once more a restriction on Satan was removed, but life was to be left inviolate. Satan filled Job's body with pain and running sores "from the sole of his foot to the crown of his head," and Job went "and sat among the ashes."

At this point Job's wife looked at him and said, "Do you still hold fast your integrity? Curse God, and die."

It was the counsel of Satan from the lips of his wife! Notice especially that the words Job's wife spoke on earth were the very words that had been spoken in heaven! Satan had said that the result of severe loss and affliction would be that Job would "curse God."

Now here—at a critical juncture in Job's trial, and also at the critical juncture in Satan's dispute with God concerning Job—comes Job's wife, standing over him and speaking the very desire of Satan! All Satan wanted was that Job curse God. If Job had sunk under his wife's counsel, Satan would have been proved right in his contention that Job worshiped God for what he got out of it.

All of her words—"Do you still hold fast your integrity? Curse God, and die"—were put into her mind and into her mouth by the prompting of Satan. Yet Job did not sin with his lips. The end of it was complete vindication for God, complete vindication for Job, and complete defeat for Satan. Satan understood now that there was a man upon the earth who loved God *solely for Himself*.

The Origin of Satan

Satan's program has always been to draw men away from God, as many as he can. He will use any means to that end, especially lies and deceptions. He will, as far as he possibly can, blur the issue, so that men will not understand that they even have a part in the conflict between God and Satan.

Every man must choose whether he will do the will of Satan or the will of God. By that choice his eternal destiny is fixed. If he does the will of Satan, he is the subject of Satan, and will spend eternity with Satan in a lake of fire that God has prepared as the place of Satan's unending punishment (Revelation 20:10). But "He who does the will of God abides forever" (1 John 2:17).

God calls men to decide. He, of course, wants them to come to Him and to enjoy eternal life. "If it seem evil to you to serve the Lord, choose you this day whom you will serve," Joshua called to the people of Israel, making the matter as immediate and urgent as he could, concluding, "As for me and my house, we will serve the Lord" (Joshua 24:15).

Satan, for all his power on the earth, is not a universal figure. He is not a kind of wicked equal to God. In his preface to *The Screwtape Letters*, C. S. Lewis put the matter well:

The commonest question is whether I really "believe in the devil." Now, if by "the devil" you mean a power opposite to God and, like God, self-existent from all eternity, the answer is certainly No. There is no uncreated being except God. God has no opposite. No being could attain a "perfect badness" opposite to the perfect goodness of God. . . . The proper question is whether I believe in devils. I do. . . . Satan, the leader or dictator of devils, is the opposite, not of God, but of Michael, the archangel.

In an allegorical description, Satan is spoken of in the Book of Job in these terms: "Upon earth there is not his like . . . *he is king over all the children of pride*" (Job 41:33, 34).

Satan was not at his origin evil at all. The one who now bears the name Satan and the title of devil was in the beginning good. The living being who became the devil was beautiful in every way.

"You had the seal of perfection, full of wisdom and perfect in beauty," Ezekiel declares. "You were in Eden, the garden of God." The passage reveals that Lucifer, or Satan, was *a created being*, full of wisdom of great beauty, perfect. "You were on the holy mountain of God. . . . You were blameless in your ways from the day you were created, until you were internally filled with violence, and you sinned" (Ezekiel 28:12-17, NAS).

This beautiful angelic being sinned. He fell into

iniquity, and was driven out of his place of high service in heaven.

"*Your heart was proud because of your beauty; you corrupted your wisdom for the sake of your splendor.*" Ezekiel thus declares by prophecy that Satan fell because he became proud of his beauty, and that he turned from serving God and began to serve his own vanity and seek his own glory.

"How art thou fallen from heaven, O Lucifer, son of the morning!

"How art thou cut down to the ground, who didst weaken the nations! *For thou hast said in thine heart, I will ascend into heaven,* I WILL EXALT MY THRONE ABOVE THE STARS OF GOD; I will sit also upon the mount of the congregation, in the sides of the north. I will ascend above the heights of the clouds; I WILL BE LIKE THE MOST HIGH.

"Yet thou shalt be brought down to hell, to the sides of the pit. They that see thee shall narrowly look upon thee, and consider thee, saying, Is this *the man who made the earth to tremble, who did shake kingdoms; who made the world as a wilderness, and destroyed the cities thereof,* who opened not the house of his prisoners?" (Isaiah 14:12-17)

Lucifer was not an ordinary servant of God, one of the ranks, so to speak. He was an extraordinary servant of God, created for and appointed to a place of leadership. It is probable that he was the messenger of God to other created beings, their angelic leader within the universal government of God. Lucifer was a creature so beautiful that he was called "the son of the morning."

But Lucifer decided, on the basis of his beauty, his exalted station, and his perfection, that he would no longer submit to being subordinate to God but that he would make the attempt to set himself above God, to depose God from His throne at the head of the universe, to overthrow His authority, and to bring God into subordination to him. That was the iniquity that was found in his heart. He wanted to take the place of God! That is still the consuming ambition of Satan.

Self-will and self-exaltation began the ruin of Satan. Five times he declared "I WILL" in express opposition to God. Each of those five times, he asserted that he would do something to promote his own interests in defiance of the interests of God.

"I will ascend to heaven.

"I will set *my throne* on high.

"I will sit on the mount of assembly in the far north.

"I will ascend above the heights of the clouds.

"I will make myself like the Most High."

That was Satan's program for himself. It was his incredibly audacious bid to overthrow the supremacy of God and to make himself the center of the universe.

He has not succeeded at that—and never will. It is an impossible ambition. But he has succeeded in becoming that evil one "who made the earth tremble, who shook kingdoms, who made the world a desert and overthrew its cities," and he is still working. Satan has succeeded in drawing intelligent beings after him in this work of destruction.

Satan is the spiritual leader of all men who do not actively, consciously, and truly worship, obey, and follow God, not in some manner that suits themselves, but in the manner that suits Him—"in spirit and in truth."

"God is a spirit," the Bible says, "and they that worship Him must worship Him in spirit and in truth" (John 4:24).

Those who indulge in sin, of whatever form, are

not the sons of God. They are the subjects of Satan.

The idea that "we are all the children of God," that all men are God's children, is not at all a biblical idea. With utter clarity, the Bible divides mankind into only two classes: the children of God, and the children of Satan.

We are not, by birth, the children of God. We inherit the nature of sin from our first father, Adam. The whole race of Adam is under the dominion and influence of Satan because of sin. We are "by nature the children of wrath" (Ephesians 2:3b).

Satan, "the god of this world," is the promulgator of the false religious teaching that "all men are the children of God." That is a lie. It stands in direct contradiction to the declaration of the Scriptures. Those who believe it understand themselves to be what, in fact, they are not.

On one occasion, Jesus spoke to a group of religious teachers who were leading the people astray and told them plainly where they stood: "*You are of your father the devil* and the lusts of your father you will do," he said (John 8:44a). "No one born of God practices sin, because His seed [God's nature] abides in him. . . . By this the children of God and the children of the devil are obvious" (1 John 3:9, 10, NAS).

Since we are not children of God by birth and by nature, we need to become the children of God. We do not have the power to make ourselves that. We become the children of God only by being "born again." That is why Jesus came: "He was in the world, and the world was made by Him, and the world knew Him not . . . But as many as received Him, to them gave He power to *become the sons of God*, . . . who were *born*, not of blood, nor of the will of the flesh, nor of the will of man, but of God" (John 1:10-13).

In presenting himself, Satan does not appear as he is, but in disguise—that is, he presents himself as what he is not. The Bible says that "Satan disguises himself as an angel of light" (2 Corinthians 11:14, NAS). He never shows himself in his true character, and he hates being shown to men in that character.

It is a triumph of Satan's policy that so little is known of him in a world in which he promotes and sponsors so much evil and destruction and death. The Bible shows the scope of his influence and power. It says quite flatly that *"the whole world lies in the power of the evil one"* (1 John 5:19b, NAS). If that has not been apparent, it is becoming more so now, and will become much more so in the years ahead.

In the activities of his rebellion against God and his bid for the destruction of man, Satan is not alone.

The Angels of the Dragon

Just as God has angels who do His will, Satan has angels who do his will. The Bible calls them evil spirits. It also calls them demons, or devils.

There is no more terrible reality confronting human existence than that of demons. Demons are the unseen enemies of God and of man; they are ceaselessly at work against the will of God and against all of the best interests of man. The effects of their activity are all around us today, and the Scriptures inform us that these effects are going to be multiplied many times, and at a very rapid pace, at the juncture in history when Israel again seeks to make herself secure in her ancient land. Yet there is no major area of biblical revelation that is more appallingly neglected.

The demons depend for success in their program of disrupting and destroying human life on ignorance of who they are, what they do, and how they do it. The Bible, the accurate guide to the who and what of the supernatural, throws the searchlight of revelation into the darkness in which demons thrive and shows them up.

The Bible tells of the origin of demons, reveals their activities and shows their destiny.

By the knowledge gained through the Word of God demons may be exposed, identified, and dispossessed by men. They may also be intelligently and effectively resisted.

As the head of an organized rebellion against the government of God, Satan leads a host of angelic collaborators. It appears that they number in the millions.

The demons were not created as such. They had their origin among the angels of God, as Satan had. Demons are reprobate angels who follow Satan and do his will.

All of the angels were servants of God until Lucifer, the "son of the morning," rebelled and caused a great split among them. Most held to their loyalty to God. Others abandoned that loyalty and went after Lucifer, or Satan.

The Scriptures speak of the angels who sinned against God. The Bible says that "God did not spare angels when they sinned, but cast them into hell and committed them to pits of darkness, reserved for judgment" (2 Peter 2:4, NAS).

Again, the Book of Jude tells of "the angels which kept not their first estate but left their own habitation" (Jude 6). The demons are angels who left their first estate, as Satan left his.

Demons are individual personalities and have names. Like all spiritual beings, demons are normally invisible to man. They possess the same faculties as angels, but they have put them to wicked ends. Every evil spirit has a will, intelligence, a personality, and a distinctive character of its own.

"Evil spirits" is an accurate descriptive term for demons because they are spirits—invisible living beings—wholly devoted to doing evil.

I have quoted the Scripture that declares that "God is a *sp rit.*" Angels are described as "ministering *spirits.*" As fallen angels, demons are described as "evil *spirits.*"

We are told that Satan, "the prince of the power of the air," is "the spirit who is at work in the children of disobedience." Notice that term "at work." It speaks of direct, personal activity by Satan upon and within individual human beings.

The work of evil spirits is to ruin men morally, spiritually, physically, and mentally.

The word angel literally means "messenger." Holy angels are messengers of God. Demons are messengers of Satan who engage in tempting men to do what is evil and in encouraging them to believe what is not true.

The Scriptures reveal that demons have "doctrines," or a system of spiritual teachings they present to men, contrary to the truth. Demons have false doctrines of salvation, of eternal destiny, of love, of reincarnation, of self-sacrifice, of asceticism, of the way of access to God, and many others besides. Each of these doctrines is a lie, presented as truth. That is why the Scriptures warn us not to be ignorant of the devil's devices and not to "give heed to spirits and doctrines of devils" (1 Timothy 4:1).

Demons—as deliberate, conscious agents of Satan—are occupied in constant, active rebellion against God.

Taken together, demons constitute the invisible forces of evil assailing mankind today—assailing individual men, societies, and nations. Their activities are increasing and will continue to increase as the great prophetic events of the end-time occur. Ignorance of who they are and what they do will become more than ever deadly. (See 1 John 4:1-3.)

The earth, and particularly the atmosphere of the earth, is under occupation by Satan and his angelic legions. That is why Satan is called "the god of this world" and "the prince of the power of the air." With him, among the demons, are other evil princes subordinate to him. They stand together in unrelenting defiance of God's will.

There is a graphic instance of this in the Book of Daniel, the Jewish prophet in the court of Babylon. To Daniel was entrusted a series of prophecies concerning the whole course of Gentile world kingdoms and concerning the destiny of the Jewish people "in the latter days."

Because of the gravity of what he was shown, Daniel devoted three full weeks to prayer and partial fasting. In response, a Visitor came to Daniel from heaven.

When this "man clothed in linen" appeared to him, Daniel writes, "I stood up trembling. Then he said to me, 'Do not be afraid, Daniel, for *from the first day* that you set your heart on understanding this and on humbling yourself before your God, your words were heard, and I have come in response to your words. But *the prince of the kingdom of Persia was withstanding me for twenty-one days;* then behold, Michael, one of the chief princes, came to help me . . . Now I have come to give you an understanding of what will happen to your people in the latter days' " (Daniel 10:11-14a, NAS).

The amazing fact is that the Visitor from heaven had trouble getting through!

Daniel's prayer was heard the *first day* and the Visitor was sent on the first day, but when He reached the atmosphere of the earth "the prince of the kingdom of Persia" arose and withstood him for 21 days. Daniel engaged in prayer and fasting that entire time.

In this passage God, angels, demons, and men are seen in related action in the conflict.

"The prince of the kingdom of Persia" who withstood the Visitor is the demonic leader of the forces of spiritual darkness in Persia. He is the chief demon appointed by Satan to rule over Persia in the interests of Satan and against the interests of God.

Notice that Michael, a chief prince of the angels of God, came to the side of the man from heaven. This visit to the earth created an emergency for "the rulers of the darkness of this world" and aroused them to a mighty effort to prevent the crucial visitation. Michael came and stood against the prince of the kingdom of Persia—a prince angel contending against a prince demon—and occupied him so that the Visitor was free to continue on His way to Daniel.

Daniel had a part in this conflict. It was his wholehearted prayer that caused the Visitor to come—"I have come in response to your words," He told Daniel—to impart vital information about the future of the Jews.

This episode from Daniel exposes the reality of the intense opposition of evil spirits to the purposes of God. We must not underestimate that conflict, for it is going on today with greater ferocity and it is beginning to affect all of us, directly or indirectly. It is beginning to affect our nation in pronounced and disquieting ways.

Chapter 7

Demons Exposed

The object of demons is to get men to do Satan's will. Demons work on men—to affect their thinking and behavior—from the outside and from the inside.

A primary function of demons is to tempt men to do evil. Demonic spirits come to a man and stand, as it were, at the gates of his consciousness. It is in their power to introduce suggestions directly into the minds of men, communicating them from their own evil imaginations to the human mind. By this means they tempt a man or they plant their own thoughts or lies in his mind. Every human being experiences that.

The demons hope, of course, for a successful transference of an evil thought from the spiritual realm into the human realm. That is how "doctrines of demons" get into circulation among mankind. A man is not obliged to accept the thought; he may sweep it aside and give it no leave to occupy his mind.

Temptation is Satan's opening wedge into a man's being. He does not want to stop there. If a man will obey demonic promptings to do evil, Satan will do worse with him by far than merely to tempt him.

In the work of soliciting men to do their master's

will, demons are not content to work outside of a man. They prefer to enter into a man and to work from inside his body.

An immensely important fact is that evil spirits can enter into and occupy the human body and use it as the vehicle for carrying out their own depraved intentions under certain circumstances. They cannot, I hasten to add, do this at just any time. They must be given a basis for occupation by voluntary acts of human compliance with the will of Satan.

Stop and read that entire statement again. It is one of the most important, yet least known, facts with which man has to do. You may have known people in that condition.

Demons in Hiding

When they work from outside, demons can appeal to and importune a man to do some sin, but they cannot make him do so. When they get inside, they obtain a measure of direct control over the man and they can use him for their own purposes. When they inhabit a human being, evil spirits become inseparably identified with the individual in whom they dwell. They are able at times to speak directly and audibly through the lips of that individual.

My awareness of this fact came first in a most unexpected way, during an interview with a seminary professor of psychiatry and religion in April 1964. I had sought the interview for a story I was doing for a magazine, but I had not anticipated its content.

After some discussion of healing in the first 300 years of the Christian church, the professor told me of a young married woman in a southern state who had become deeply disturbed in her personality, for reasons that were not apparent. She had been to psychologists but had obtained no help. Later she sought the help of a minister, who took a radically different approach to her case and through whose help she obtained relief from her distress, relief that had proved to be lasting.

"I have a tape recording," the professor said, "of the session in which the young woman got relief from her trouble. It is quite remarkable. Would you like to hear it?"

In the next 45 minutes, what was to me an entirely new dimension of understanding of an important aspect of the spiritual and supernatural realm began to unfold. As the tape went round, I heard two voices. The voice of the minister and the woman's voice. But it shortly became plain that the minister was not talking to the woman. He was talking to *another intelligent personality who was in the woman!* He was addressing himself, intentionally and directly, to an evil spirit.

What I remember most vividly is that, about halfway through the session, the woman's voice changed. It ceased to be a natural young woman's voice and became an odd, rather high-pitched, whiny, nasal sound.

"You're hurting my head, pastor," her voice said with a kind of nasty, pleading petulance. Three or four times the phrase was repeated.

"I am not touching this young woman's head. I am not hurting her head. I am speaking to you, you foul and lying spirit," the minister said. Two or three times he reproved the evil spirit for lying through the woman's lips.

As I realized later, the demon to whom the minister was speaking was being brought out of hiding by stages—was, in short, through God's superior power beginning to be forced against its will to reveal itself as actually present in the young woman.

Up to that point, the evil spirit had sought to hide its identity entirely behind that of the woman and to remain undetected. Now, however, the evil spirit knew that it had been discovered and identified by the minister, and it began to speak directly, with no further attempt to hide.

For a while this intruding personality was rather belligerent, but as the minister took authority over it, an evident tremor came into the voice that spoke to the minister and it increased until its tone was that of almost hysterical panic.

"You are going to go out of this young woman," the minister said in a strong, even voice.

"If I go out, I will come back in," the high-pitched voice replied.

"No. You will not come back in," the minister said. "You are going to go out today and you will never come back in."

All challenges, all argument disappeared from the responding voice. The voice became considerably weaker, and it was filled with fear and pleading. The evil spirit to whom the minister spoke no longer made an issue of staying or leaving. Instead, it began to bargain for the terms of its departure! The voice begged the minister, in a pitiful manner, not to command it to go to Jerusalem.

The minister took final authority. "You foul and lying spirit," he said, "I command you, in the name of Jesus Christ, to come out of this woman now and not to return."

The young woman, from that moment on, had suffered no more from her perplexing distress, the professor said. He said that what I heard had taken place some months earlier.

This was a modern-day instance of the casting out of demons. It was the first of which I had ever known, but in the next several years I was to learn of case after case from many different sources, all isolated but often exhibiting the most striking similarities in method, in response and result. It became impossible for me to avoid the conclusion that evil spirits exist and that they sometimes enter into human beings, entirely unsuspected and unseen, and remain until something explicit and forceful and direct is done to get them out.

That conclusion was not easier for me to reach, I think, than for you, but I would ask you not to close your mind or to decide about it until you have read what comes in the pages just ahead.

In the past five years I have heard, from the lips of reputable and intelligent ministers and missionaries, so many accounts of their own direct experiences in dealing with evil spirits that had taken up residence within troubled individuals—and these accounts, though they were based on experiences as far removed as China and Switzerland, are so remarkably similar in their content—that I cannot doubt their validity.

Demons Exposed

While on a reporting trip through the Midwest I met an Episcopal rector in Illinois, who told me of a singular experience in his ministry.

The Rev. Richard E. Winkler said that the six-year-old son of a woman who lived near the church had become dangerously destructive, but physicians could find no cause nor offer any solution. The boy would sometimes strike matches and set fires and he would jump out of the second-story window of his home, bruising himself in the drop.

The boy's mother brought him to the church. "The mother was beside herself," the rector said.

"She had to watch the child every moment. Evidently he was possessed by demons of destruction."

As soon as he took the child and put him on his lap the boy kicked and thrashed and struggled like a wild animal. The rector had to hold him down. While several others prayed, the minister began to deal directly with an evil spirit of destruction. He took authority over the evil spirit and, in the name of Jesus Christ, ordered it to leave the child.

"It was wonderful to see," the minister's wife said. "The child changed just like night and day, from a kicking, squalling kid to a peaceful, quiet little boy before our eyes." Now calm and still, the boy needed no longer to be held.

Mr. Winkler said that the child had never since set fires or done anything else abnormally destructive. He appeared to be a normal, happy child thereafter.

"The demons recognize what's going to happen," Mr. Winkler said. "They make a final, desperate bid to hold on to their human victim or, failing that, to harm him."

The rector also told of a church member who had "a daughter who was normal until her college years but something happened in college and she became possessed with several kinds of demons. The mother brought the girl to the altar and when we gathered around to pray for her, the demons threw her to the floor three or four times," before they finally departed.

It is important to recognize that Jesus did not deal with the evil spirits as *conditions* but as with *intelligent beings.*

There are some who say that, in this, Jesus was merely ceding something to the superstitions of His time, but it is not the case. Jesus made a distinction between a condition—as in certain illnesses—and

demonic possession, and He dealt with conditions
as conditions, and He dealt with evil spirits as evil
spirits, and He knew the difference. Some illnesses
He healed as illnesses; others He recognized as
physical symptoms of demon possession and He
cast the evil spirits out. To confound the two is to
leave some people, strangely afflicted or tormented
or unbalanced, without hope of relief. To confound
the two is also to confuse the matter in a way that is
convenient to the hope of demons to remain undetected.

In the case of the Gadarene demoniac (cf. Mark
5), Jesus confronted a man with an unclean spirit
who lived in a cemetery who was so strong that "no
man could bind him, no, not with chains: for he had
often been bound with fetters and chains, and the
chains he had plucked asunder . . . neither could
any man tame him . . . always, night and day, he
was in the tombs, crying and cutting himself with
stones."

As soon as Jesus and the man saw each other,
there was a two-way recognition. The evil spirits in
the man recognized Jesus, and Jesus recognized the
evil spirits.

The man's voice cried out, "What do I have to do
with You, Jesus, Son of the Most High God?—the
demons knew exactly who stood before them—"I
implore You by God, do not torment me!"

As soon as He met him, Jesus fixed His gaze on
the man in the tombs and said, "Come out of the
man, you unclean spirit!"

It is critically important to notice that Jesus *did
not address the man*. He went *beyond the man* and
directly addressed the unclean spirit.

It was not the man speaking. It was the demons
speaking, trying to hide themselves behind the
identity of the man, to make it appear that the man

was speaking. Evil spirits seek the closest possible identification with the person they inhabit, so that their words and acts will be mistakenly ascribed to the person.

There is more here than the speech of a man. There was instant recognition, not only of Jesus as a man, but of Jesus as the "Son of the Most High God." Men may not know that Jesus is the Son of God—some do, most do not—but every demon knows who Jesus is. They have no uncertainty whatever about it. The Bible says that "the devils also believe, and tremble" (James 2:19b).

In this case, the evil spirits were in great fear of Jesus, because He had absolute power over them, so they begged Him not to torment them.

Up to this point they used the first person singular because they still hoped to conceal their true identity. They hoped to make it seem that the *man* was asking Jesus not to torment him.

Plainly, Jesus had not come to torment the man. It was the demons who were doing that.

Jesus did not speak to the man, but He went beyond the man and addressed the demons: "What is your name?"

"My name is Legion," the man's voice answered, "for *we* are many."

The demons, knowing that they had been discovered, changed abruptly from the first person singular to the plural. They were now out in the open, forced to reveal themselves as foreign beings inhabiting the body of the man.

This abrupt switch of terms is quite typical in cases where evil spirits are being dealt with directly. For a while they will speak only of "I" and "me," then suddenly they will refer to the individual they are occupying as "him" or "her," thus making the distinction between themselves and their victim. Or they will speak of "we" and "us." This occurs when they are flushed out of hiding and made to reveal themselves as separate identities.

Mark 5:12 of this account specifically reveals that it was not the possessed man who was speaking to Jesus, but the unclean spirits in the man. It says: "They *entreated* Him, saying, 'Send us into the swine so that we may enter them'" (NAS).

Jesus made them leave the man, but He allowed them to go into the swine. Immediately two things happened.

The man out of whom the demons had gone sat there quietly, "clothed and *in his right mind.*"

The pigs, however, immediately "rushed down the steep bank into the sea." The herd ran wild, and 2,000 swine were drowned.

Real demons had gone out of a real man and entered real pigs. When they left the man and went into the pigs, their activity was transferred from the man to the pigs. There could be no more graphic depiction of the reality of demons and of the effects of demon possession.

King Saul

Demons work to produce definite effects in human thought and behavior. Such effects can be seen in the life of Saul, the first king of Israel. He was, the Bible affirms, "a choice young man"—humble, gentle, exceedingly good-looking.

The prophet Samuel anointed him for the office. Soon after this anointing, "the Spirit of God came upon him, and he [Saul] prophesied" (1 Samuel 10:10).

The young king was greatly blessed by God. He was a modest and unassuming individual, but he was weak and only partial in his obedience to God.

He began well but, through cumulative acts of disobedience, Saul lost the blessing. The fateful transition is seen in 1 Samuel 16:14:

"But the Spirit of the Lord departed from Saul, and an evil spirit from the Lord troubled him."

The course, which had tended upward, now ran steeply downward. Saul ended as a man capable of murder. At the very end, he sank to consulting a medium and that brought swift death to him.

God withdrew His Holy Spirit from Saul and allowed an evil spirit to go to him. This change in the spiritual realm brought distinct and drastic changes in Saul's behavior. The first effect was that the evil spirit "troubled him," causing Saul to suffer internal agitation and unrest.

"And Saul's servants said to him, 'Behold now, an evil spirit from God troubles you. Let the king now command his servants . . . to seek out a man who is a cunning player on an harp, and it shall come to pass, when the evil spirit from God is upon you, that he shall play with his hand, and you shall be well.' "

The one selected for this service was a young man named David. "And David came to Saul and stood before him, and Saul loved him greatly; and David became his armor-bearer" (1 Samuel 16:15, 16, 21).

Saul's immediate reaction to David was that he loved him greatly. But soon, under the incendiary influences of the demon, he would show an entirely different aspect.

As young David began to become a respected warrior for Israel, Saul felt the stirrings of jealousy and anger within him. . . . "Now it came about on the next day that an evil spirit from God came mightily upon Saul, and he raved in the midst of the house, while David was playing the harp with his hand, as usual; and a spear was in Saul's hand. And Saul hurled the spear, for he thought, 'I will pin David to the wall.' But David escaped from his presence twice" (1 Samuel 18:10, 11, NAS).

The man who a short while before had held David in great affection made two impulsive attempts to murder him. If he had killed David he would perhaps have said when asked why—as others have said: "I don't know. Something came over me."

Anger, jealousy, rage, hatred, fear, the impulse to murder—all these were produced in the life of Saul by the activity of the evil spirit.

The last step for Saul was a deliberate and desperate encounter with occultism. When Saul had been pursuing the will of God he "had put the mediums and wizards out of the land," because God had commanded that these demonic substitutes have no part in the pure worship of the Jews.

"And the Philistines gathered . . . And when Saul saw the host of the Philistines, he was afraid. . . . And when Saul enquired of the Lord, the Lord answered him not. . . . Then said Saul to his servants, 'Seek me a woman who is a medium, that I may go to her, and enquire of her.' And his servants said, 'There is a woman who is a medium at Endor.'

"So Saul disguised himself, and put on other clothing, and he went . . . and said (to the woman), 'Divine unto me . . . and bring me up whom I shall name'" (1 Samuel 28:4-8).

Consulting a medium is a shortcut to getting the counsel of Satan upon a matter, though that counsel is usually carefully disguised so that it will not appear to be what it is.

"On the morrow, when the Philistines came to strip the slain, they found Saul and his three sons fallen on Mount Gilboa" (1 Samuel 31:8).

It was but hours between Saul's visit to the medium and his death. He had stepped past the point of no return.

Hear the Word of God: "As for the person who turns to mediums and to spirits, to play the harlot after them, I will also set My face against that person and will cut him off from among his people" (Leviticus 20:6, NAS). Whatever the come-on, the payoff can be death.

Casting Demons Out

God has provided the means and the power by which demons inhabiting human beings can be expelled. The Bible speaks of certain "spiritual gifts" that God has given to empower men to engage effectively in the conflict against Satan and the demons.

In his first letter to the Corinthians, the Apostle Paul wrote, "Now concerning spiritual gifts, brethren, I do not want you to be unaware" (1 Corinthians 12:1, NAS). In this same chapter, Paul lists nine specific spiritual gifts imparted by the Holy Spirit.

Among the nine is one that has specifically to do with demons. It is the gift of the "discerning of spirits." This gift has been excellently defined as "the God-given ability to detect the presence and ascertain the identity of evil spirits."

The individual to whom this gift is given is enabled first to recognize that evil spirits are present in an individual and second to identify them specifically and to deal with them directly.

The gift has nothing whatever to do with natural insight; it is not in any sense an activity or product of the human mind. It is entirely spiritual in its operation and it is a gift of revelation. The gift comes directly from God by the Holy Spirit to an individual and, by it, God reveals to the individual the presence and the identity of evil spirits dwelling in human victims. The purpose of the gift is to make it possible for persons who are afflicted or tormented by demons to be set free.

The name, i.e., the authority, of Jesus is the only power that can conquer demons and cast them out. Evil spirits cannot be dealt with effectively in any other way. Moreover, the name of Jesus and His authority over evil spirits can only be applied and enforced by an individual who truly believes in Him.

There is an interesting account in the Book of Acts regarding this. "God was performing extraordinary miracles by the hands of Paul," by which some who were sick were healed and others who had evil spirits were set free. "But also some of the Jewish exorcists, who went from place to place, attempted to name over those who had the evil spirits the name of the Lord Jesus, saying, 'I adjure you by Jesus whom Paul preaches.'

"And seven sons of one Sceva, a Jewish chief priest, were doing this. And *the evil spirit answered and said to them,* 'I recognize Jesus, and I know about Paul, but who are you?' And the man in whom was the evil spirit leaped on them and subdued . . . them and overpowered them, so that they fled out of that house naked and wounded" (Acts 19:11-16, NAS).

One man, possessed with a demon, overcame seven young men. You will recall that while the legion of demons possessed the man in the tombs, he had more than merely human strength and "no one had the strength to subdue him."

The mistake of the seven young men was that they attempted to engage in a supernatural activity by imitation. It was a secondhand sort of thing.

They did not know Jesus personally, but by reputation. Their use of His name was therefore of no effect.

There is no magic in invoking the name of Jesus in exorcism, but there is power to cast demons out in His name when it is spoken by one who knows Jesus and who has the gift of discerning of spirits and the ministry of casting them out.

In the casting out of demons, the attitude of the person in whom the demons dwell is of utmost importance.

The Scripture gives the reason for this. Jesus, whose understanding of the work of demons was perfect, said, "When the unclean spirit goes out of a man, it passes through waterless places, seeking rest, and does not find it. Then it says, 'I will return to my house from which I came;' and when it comes, it finds it unoccupied, swept, and put in order. Then it goes, and takes along with it seven other spirits more wicked than itself, and they go in and live there; and *the last state of that man becomes worse than the first*" (Matthew 12:43-45, NAS).

A man becomes demon-possessed chiefly through his own sin. If he does not truly repent of the sin and turn from it, by the power of Jesus Christ, the demon who is cast out will return, bringing other demons with him. In a man with a propensity to anger there is no point in casting out the demon of anger until it is certain that the man desires to be rid of the sin of anger. If the sin, which gave the demon occasion in the first place, persists, the demon of anger will return, often with reinforcements.

On the other hand, if the man turns decisively from the sin and refuses again to engage in it, the casting out of the demon will set him free permanently.

Chapter 8

The Thieves of Forever

At the time in Israel's history when Elijah had arisen as one of the mightiest prophets and workers of miracles the nation had known, Jezebel ruled as queen in Israel. She was a Gentile. Though she practiced idolatry and worshiped a false god, Ahab, the king, had taken her as his wife. Jezebel was far the stronger personality, and her weak husband ceded much of the management of affairs into her hands.

Ahab thereby threw open the gates of Israel to false worship, bringing grief upon the nation and judgment upon himself. "Ahab did more to provoke the Lord God of Israel to anger than all the kings of Israel that were before him" (1 Kings 16:33).

Jezebel pursued a bloody career in Israel. Her chief instrument of policy was murder. Since she sat at the head of government, it was easy for her to put this policy into official and fiercely effective operation. She had but to give the order, and the sword of government struck.

There was no political opposition of any consequence in Israel at the time, so her murders did not even have the color of political self-protection. They were the wanton acts of a depraved nature. Yet what is particularly significant is that her murders and threats of murder were not the product of some burning, generalized lust to kill. Like Saul's assaults upon David, they had a specific target. They were aimed chiefly at individuals who served the God of Israel and occupied essential positions as His spokesmen to the people.

Jezebel was, to put it in its accurate spiritual perspective, the human expression of an evil will set against God's will. The queen was a woman through whom Satan could express, in the practical mode of murder, his furious hatred of God's designs.

The intimate relationship between the evil desires of Satan and the evil acts of men is seen in Jesus' denunciation of certain leaders, to whom He said: "You are of your father the devil, and the lusts of your father *you will do*. He was a murderer from the beginning" (John 8:44). Satan's lusts become men's deeds.

Satan is identified as "a murderer from the beginning." Murder lies in his very nature. Evil spirits are much involved in stirring up murder in human society.

When possible, Satan inflames individuals who hold the authority of government to carry out murders, because that is the most efficient means and it is the hardest to resist or escape. In our century Hitler became such an instrument, with a spiritual animus aimed straight at a specific target—the people whom God has called His "chosen." If it had been possible, he would have carried out Satan's historic purpose of expunging the Jewish people, as Haman had once attempted to do (Esther 3).

When Jezebel got power, one of her earliest acts was a venture in mass murder. The first Book of Kings records that "Jezebel cut off the prophets of the Lord . . . , Jezebel killed the prophets of the Lord" (1 Kings 18:4, 13).

Elijah escaped, and another hundred prophets found refuge in a cave. These survivors lived in fear of their lives and could not move freely.

Later, following the crucial supernatural contest on Mount Carmel in which Elijah called down fire from heaven and commanded the slaying of false prophets who had flooded Israel under Jezebel's patronage, Jezebel sent a messenger to Elijah to inform him that she had sworn that he would be slain "by this time tomorrow." She seemed to be in a position to carry out her threat. Elijah fled.

A man named Naboth owned a vineyard near the palace of King Ahab. The king wanted it for use as a vegetable garden. Ahab offered to exchange it for another vineyard or to buy it from Naboth at fair market value. "But Naboth said to Ahab, 'The Lord forbid me that I should give you the inheritance of my fathers.' So Ahab came into his house sullen and vexed. . . . But Jezebel his wife came to him and said to him, 'How is it that your spirit is so sullen that you are not eating food? . . . Do you now reign over Israel? Arise, eat bread, and let your heart be joyful; *I will give you the vineyard of Naboth the Jezreelite.*'

"So she wrote letters in Ahab's name and sealed them with his seal," directing that Naboth be invited to a certain event and that two false witnesses be planted among the guests to accuse him of something he had not done. Soon, the desired word reached Jezebel: " 'Naboth has been stoned, and is dead.' " Jezebel said to Ahab, " 'Arise, take possession of the vineyard of Naboth . . . for Naboth is not alive, but dead' " (1 Kings 21, NAS).

When Ahab went down to take possession of the slain man's vineyard—breaking the tenth commandment: "neither shall you covet your neighbor's house, his field . . . or anything that is your neighbor's"—the Lord Himself watched and swiftly acted.

"The word of the Lord came to Elijah the Tishbite, saying, 'Arise, go down and meet Ahab king of Israel . . . behold, he is in the vineyard of Naboth . . . And you shall speak to him, saying, 'Thus says the Lord, "In the place where the dogs licked up the blood of Naboth the dogs shall lick up your blood.' "

"Ahab said to Elijah, 'Have you found me, O my enemy?' And he answered, 'I have found you, because *you have sold yourself to do evil in the sight of the Lord'* " (from 1 Kings 21, NAS).

The Bible warns that those "who take the sword shall perish by the sword." That law was put into effect in the case of Ahab, the man who sold himself to do evil. By his marriage to Jezebel, Ahab rapidly heathenized Israel.

In taking to himself a woman thoroughly devoted to things God had forbidden, Ahab opened a breach in Israel through which the will of Satan gained astonishing ascendancy.

Jezebel's link to Satan was through the false religion and false worship. Her involvement with these things had made her an active enemy of God.

The death of sinners is a harvest for Satan. That is why Isaiah writes, referring to a time when death stalked Israel because of famine and drought, "hell has enlarged herself and opened her mouth without measure" to swallow men (Isaiah 5:13,14).

At the moment of death, the state and destiny of a man's soul is fixed forever, beyond the slightest possibility of change. Evil spirits know that. They therefore work to keep a man from reconciliation to God throughout his lifetime. They also seek to spread death so that human lifetimes are cut short.

Every form of murder removes souls from life and brings them to judgment. As the Scripture says, "it is appointed unto men once to die, but after this the judgment" (Hebrews 9:27).

The powers of evil under Satan work incessantly to produce murder in human society. At times, murder arises in a kind of mad wave and sweeps through populations, leaving thousands, sometimes millions, dead.

We were appalled in 1969 to witness that obstinate stalemate of wills by which tens of thousands of Biafrans suffered starvation in a politically induced famine.

Apart from wars, waves of murder have arisen in this present century in Europe under Nazism, in Russia under Bolshevism and, more recently, in China in the mass executions during the first years of the Maoist regime and then, in the latter half of the 1960s in that violent and evil spasm, the great revolution of the Red Guards. In each of these events, evil spirits were at work to produce human slaughter.

Murder Exported from the Supernatural Order

Sir Basil Zaharoff, one of the most honored and one of the most evil men of his time, specialized in contriving wars among states and prolonging them.

A book was published in 1965 titled *Peddler of Death: The Life and Times of Sir Basil Zaharoff* by Donald McCormick. A concise and lucid summary in *Newsweek* said: "Like many legendary empire builders, slum-born Basil Zaharoff started simply but shrewdly. In the 1880s he sold the navy-scarce Greeks one of his firm's revolutionary new warships. Then, drachmas in hand, he warned Greece's Turkish enemies of the purchase, offering them two submarines. Next, warning Russia of the danger to her Black Sea ports, Zaharoff sold Russia four more subs to cancel the Greek and Turkish threats he had created. . . .

"Though Zaharoff rose to society's highest stations, no chicanery was beneath him . . . Zaharoff's incredible business brain excelled at crushing or compromising competitors, negotiating clandestine alliances and creating his own markets in the form of arms scares or actual wars.

"Zaharoff held 300 business directorates and received 298 decorations from 31 nations . . . He employed a network of spies that included high government officials, trigger men, and flunkies specializing not only in bribery, blackmail and murder, but also in respectability.

" 'I could have shown the Allies three points at which, had they struck, the enemy's armaments potential could have been utterly destroyed,' he boasted during the war. 'But that would have ruined the business.'

". . . When Britain's Lloyd George allowed Zaharoff to engineer the Greek invasion of Turkey, the disastrous defeat costing 100,000 Greek lives brought the Prime Minister's government crashing down. . . . When he died in 1936, Zaharoff was a lonely, reviled man. 'Millions died that he might live,' said an obituary."

Evil spirits found a man, a lover of money and power, with great ability and large vision, who did not scruple to maneuver nations toward war by artful manipulations on the highest levels. Zaharoff brought death by violence to countless thousands of his fellowmen. What the prophet Elijah said to the wicked King Ahab of Israel, "You have sold yourself to do evil in the sight of the Lord," could be said of such a man as this (1 Kings 21:20b, NAS).

Now consider a young man who lost his faith and discovered pleasure in bringing death.

TRAINED TO HEAL, GI DOCTOR SAYS "I LOVE TO KILL" was the arresting headline on a story from Saigon by Georgie Anne Geyer of the *Chicago Daily News*. She told this story (condensed here): "I met this congenial young captain—we'll call him Capt. Bob Miller—one night in a coastal city in Vietnam. A doctor, he had been assigned for a year to a combat unit in a forward area. Now his time was over, and he sat in one of those dark, depressingly garish officers' bars and talked unhappily about his future.

" 'If I stay on, they'll put me in a rear hospital,' he complained, 'and then I won't see combat. So I've talked with this buddy of mine, and we're thinking of becoming mercenaries and finding another war.'

" 'Mercenaries?' I asked. 'You'd leave your wife . . . ?'

" 'I don't know if I will, but I certainly would,' he answered. His face was thoughtful, determined. It was a square, wholesome American face, topped by a crewcut.

" 'I finally found myself in combat,' he went on. 'I love it. I love to kill. You see, I never knew what I could do before. I was never able to pit myself against anything and really try myself out. Now I know. That's why I love war.'

"He paused and mused, 'You know what my shield would be?' he asked finally. I couldn't imagine. 'A clenched fist,' he answered, 'sinking under the waves with lightning and thunder crashing all around it.'

"Capt. Miller told me how he had been raised in a strict fundamentalist church, and how he had lost faith when he went to college. It was a great loss for him, and he never quite got over it."

This is the story of a man who had been filled with the lust to destroy: "I love to kill . . . I love war." The young physician had become a friend—and instrument—of death.

From the diary of Ernst Jünger comes this description of the last German offensive in 1918:

"The great moment had come. The curtain of fire lifted from the front trenches. We stood up . . . we moved in step, ponderously but irresistibly toward the enemy lines. . . . My right hand embraced the shaft of my pistol, my left a riding stick of bamboo cane. I was boiling with a mad rage, which had taken hold of me and all the others in an incomprehensible fashion. The overwhelming wish to kill gave wings to my feet. Rage pressed bitter tears from my eyes. . . . The monstrous desire for annihilation, which hovered over the battlefield, thickened the brains of the men and submerged them in a red fog. We called to each other in sobs and stammered disconnected sentences. A neutral observer might have perhaps believed that we were seized by an excess of happiness."

Evan S. Connell, Jr., commenting on this, wrote: "When a soldier drifts into such a condition . . . he is no longer cognizant of fighting to protect his home and family and Preserve the Faith; instead, he is obsessed by a need to kill and to desecrate. Nothing else matters. His concern is no longer with preservation but with annihilation. He despises the world. He renounces his privileges as a human for the deep joy of destruction."

This account reveals nothing less than the presence of possibly thousands of evil spirits gathered in the air at the site of battle, determined to turn it into a scene of maximum carnage. "The monstrous desire for annihilation . . . hovered over the battlefield." It "thickened the minds of the men and submerged them in a red fog." Satan's policy of death had been put into peculiarly intensive effect, at a moment when the opportunity for bringing death to many men was ripe, by a concentration of evil spirits—spirits of destruction—at the scene of battle.

Influence or Control

Satan wants human beings to think his thoughts and do his deeds. The mission of demons is to accomplish that.

What demons aim at specifically is obtaining either *influence* or *control* over the thoughts, the beliefs, and the actions of human beings. Influence is what demons seek to get when they are outside a man. Control is what they begin to get when they enter into a man.

In the world's affairs, the actual carrying out of the will of God or the will of Satan on earth depends upon human choice. When men do what Satan bids them do, they soon get Satan's results in their society. When men obey the will of God, the blessings of God flow into a society through them.

In their effort to get him to do the will of their master, demons come up against man's freedom to choose. Initially, therefore, evil spirits must resort to tactics of persuasion, since they are not able to force a man to sin.

The ultimate aim is to draw an individual so far into sin—into the habit of yielding himself to the will of Satan—that he cannot get back out.

Demons specialize in exporting evil from the supernatural to the natural plane as massively as men will permit. There are no limits to which the demons are not willing to go, if men will let them. Where the Word of God is ignored or disobeyed, they can deposit wickedness and distress in ever greater measures upon a society until at last that society is overwhelmed by evil. The same can be true of an individual life.

In Satan's program for man, lies and temptations are quite often presented together. Evil spirits know that a person who first accepts a lie is more likely to sink under a temptation. A lie softens a man up for sin.

This is a classic technique that Satan has used throughout human history. It can be seen first in his approach to the woman in Eden. It is important to realize that Satan had *no part* in man's affairs up to that point. He desired to gain an entrance into those affairs. What Satan needed was to get the woman to disobey God and to obey him, so that, through her, he might begin to have influence in the world.

The first thing Satan did was to plant a doubt in the woman's mind concerning what God had actually said. Then he told her a lie.

The way Satan took with Eve to get her to do his will is almost exactly the way he will take with us.

Satan's move, in any nation where the Word of God is in the possession of the people, is to attack the veracity and validity of the Scriptures. The truths in them stand, when they are appropriated, as a mighty bulwark against all his devices. If he can undermine the people's confidence and trust in the Scriptures, he can eventually do with the population as he wills.

The attack on the Word of God comes in strategic centers and it is particularly directed at the youth, because Satan knows that, if he can beguile new generations from truth and lead them into sin, he can, before long, wreck a nation. These strategic centers are particularly universities and seminaries —universities because they are the prime source of most of the most influential people of the next generation, seminaries because that is where ministers and preachers are trained. If you can sabotage belief there you will soon have the pulpits of denominations filled with men who have no sure standard of righteousness to proclaim to the people, men who cannot distinguish that which is holy from that which is vile. "If the blind lead the blind," Jesus said, "both shall fall into the ditch" (Matthew 15:14).

The Limitation of Demons

Men overcome Satan by loyalty to God and obedience to His word.

Only the nation in which the Bible is honored and believed will fully escape domination by one form of evil or another. *The nation that will not follow God will finally follow demons.*

Demons work on men in practical ways to involve them in sin and to keep them from God, but demons are not free to do just anything they want at any time. The range of their options and the area of their discretionary activities is very broad, but it is not unlimited.

There are limitations that are set upon them by God, and there are limitations that may be set upon them by men. If it were not the case, they would long ago have succeeded in making an entire chaos out of civilization.

If a lion were placed in a large, fenced preserve, he would be free to attack in any direction but his freedom would end abruptly at the fences of the preserve. He would be free within set limits.

That is somewhat the case with Satan and the demons. They cannot go a fraction beyond limits set on them by God, and God can, and sometimes does, either forbid them to do certain things or command them to do certain things. In that sense Satan and the demons remain subject to God.

Satan is, at the moment, having a kind of heyday in America. He is succeeding in promoting crime, sexual indulgence, perversions, violence, occultism, and civil strife to a degree that was impossible until quite recently. Thus his destructive purposes are being carried out upon individuals and groups of men, especially the young, in progressively larger ways.

For a very long time Satan softened up the nation for the present moral and spiritual attack by drawing the Bible and its powerful words further and further away from the center of American life. One of the last steps in this long process was to get the Scriptures out of the public schools.

With the Bible's hugely beneficial influence cast aside—its words are an exhortation to virtue and a restraint to sin—Satan is able to promote evil in a way that is both more widespread and more extreme than heretofore. For the "Thou shalt not's . . ." of Mount Sinai, we now have the "Do what thou wilt" of the devil.

There is no apparent sign of any reversal of this swift deteriorative process in our society. Unless there is a dramatic reversal, a large-scale repentance and turning to God, demon activity will increase steadily and become more and more obvious, open, and pronounced in its debilitative and convulsive effects in the United States.

The tide of idolatry, immorality, impurity, lawlessness, perversion, and false supernaturalism comes upon a people after they have been persuaded to trade in the truth of God for a lie, and that is happening in America today.

It can be stopped.

The limitation of Satan's power on earth is based

on a joining together of the will of God and the will of man. When that union is lacking, Satan can do nearly anything he pleases (even to organizing such advanced civilizations as those of Germany and China for national ventures in madness). When that union is present, Satan is hindered or thwarted in carrying out his will.

God is always searching for a man who will stand with Him in the crises of the world's affairs.

Moses and Gideon were not mighty men in themselves, yet they did mighty deeds in history. God summoned Moses to be His spokesman to the whole Jewish people, and to the whole court of Egypt. Moses had definite limitations that unfitted him for the job and he shrank from it. Moses was hesitant, "slow of speech and of tongue," and meek (Exodus 4:10-12; Numbers 12:3). But the Lord said, "Now therefore go, and *I will be with your mouth.*"

God was not interested in what Moses could do for Him. God was interested in what He could do *through* Moses. The work of Moses could never be explained in terms of what Moses was. It was Who was with Moses that really counted.

Gideon had behaved very timidly in the face of the enemy. He had no qualifications to be a military leader. Yet God called him to occupy that role and, by placing his whole reliance on God, Gideon overmastered enemy leaders who had vastly larger forces with much experience in battle.

I know a man who stutters. God called him to preach. He cannot keep himself from stuttering at times in conversation, but he never stutters when he preaches. God often calls men, not at the point of their strength, but at the point of the greatest weakness. By that they discover the key to the wonderful paradox of the Apostle Paul, who said, God's "strength is made perfect in [human] weakness . . .

for when I am weak, then am I strong" (2 Corinthians 12:9, 10b).

In the conflict between God and Satan, the man who gives himself most wholeheartedly to God is most useful to God in bringing forth His will in the earth. The man who gives himself most completely to sin is most useful to Satan in producing evil in the earth.

The power of Satan does not begin to be broken in a society until there arises a man, or a group of men, willing to risk everything and stake everything on the Word and the will of God. God desires to have a people in the earth through whom His truth shall triumph *by their obedience.*

Such individuals cannot be suborned by any offer —not for job, for security, nor for life itself. Satan falls before such men, for they have no price.

Men of this sort are free to hurl truth in the teeth of popular lies, to call sin by its rightful name, to defy demagogues.

Martin Luther showed this quality. "Let goods and kindred go, this mortal life also. The body they may kill, God's truth abideth still," he wrote in his glorious hymn, "A Mighty Fortress Is Our God."

"Here I stand, I can do no other," Luther declared in exalting truth above ecclesiastical tradition. Fear of death could not deter him. That is why he became such a force in breaking an age-long night of religious darkness in Europe. He dared to stand on nothing but the truth of God, in the face of massive traditions to the contrary and massive opposition. Luther knew that in this he stood against more than men. "And though this world with devils filled should threaten to undo us," he wrote, "we will not fear for God has willed His truth to triumph through us."

Chapter 9

Spirit, Soul, Body

The Greeks had one great motto for their intellectual pursuits: Know thyself. The love of wisdom—philosophy—has been praised as the highest form of human achievement through the centuries. Yet neither the Greeks with their many philosophies, nor any of the succeeding nations that engaged in this pursuit of wisdom, from the Romans to our own day, have been able to find this understanding of self.

Since the first man lost his communion with God through sin and thereby lost a true understanding of himself and his reason for being, and since all attempts by man to reach this understanding (who am I, where did I come from, why am I here, and where do I go?) have so obviously failed, the question arises whether it is at all possible for man to understand himself.

There is a way. What man cannot find out, God has chosen to reveal to him.

The Bible says, *"For what man knows the things of a man, save the spirit of man which is in him?"* (1 Corinthians 2:11).

In these words we are given the clear beginning of an understanding of man. In form the verse is a question, but actually it is a statement of an essential fact. The verse tells us that what cannot be imparted to us by our minds can be given to us by another faculty. A man cannot know the things of a man by the mind, but he can know by "the spirit of man which is in him."

It is of great importance to understand the make-up of man, the structure of his being.

God created man in His own image, therefore man is tripartite or, more accurately, triune: spirit, soul, and body. In closing his first letter to the Thessalonians, Paul wrote: "I pray God your whole *spirit* and *soul* and *body* be preserved blameless" (1 Thessalonians 5:23).

That is the sum of what man is. Fail to understand this and it can be guaranteed that you will fail to understand the nature of man.

You may ask what makes it so vital for a man to have this understanding. There are several reasons. Satan is always working to keep man deceived about himself, because by such common deceptions he is able to keep millions of men in bondage and under the power of sin. Some men are drawn, in the vanity of their minds, to estimate man above his true station, even to magnify man against God. Others are led to take such a diminished view of man that they refuse to believe that God would take an interest in such a lowly creature. Either extreme denies man a true understanding of himself. Either extreme denies him an understanding of himself in relationship to God.

To understand how evil spirits work to undermine human well-being, it is necessary to have some grasp of the nature of man: the nature of man as God intended him to be, and the nature of man as he is.

If you were to get a wrong set of instructions with a mechanism with which you were unfamiliar, your understanding of it would not correspond to

the actual nature of the thing itself. A wrong understanding of the nature of man—even when that understanding is satisfyingly complex and apparently
profound—can, when it is applied in an effort to
help a man, do him little good, and it may do him
considerable harm.

In this, the good *intentions* of the one attempting
to help are of little moment; what really counts is
the *accuracy of his understanding*.

Shakespeare was moved to write the exclamatory
phrase, "What a piece of work is a man!" Man is, indeed, an incomparable piece of work, created in the
image of God, and the Bible teaches that he is:
Spirit. Soul. Body.

It is no accident that Paul mentioned the three
major constituents of man in this order, for that
order places them in their right relationships to
each other. The progression as he gives it—spirit,
soul, body—proceeds from the innermost to the
outermost parts of a man.

For a crude illustration, we might think of a
peach. The very core of the peach is the nut, which
is surrounded by the pit, which in turn is surrounded by the fruit flesh—corresponding in this order to
spirit, soul and body. The soul is set within the
body, and the spirit is set within the soul.

The spirit is the very core of man. It is in the
spirit that man has his God-given capacity to com-
mune with God, who is Spirit, and who must be
worshiped in spirit and in truth. It is the shrine in
which spiritual life is lived.

The spirit expresses itself through the soul. The
soul, in turn, expresses itself through the physical
body. The body is the outer man, the soul is the
inner man, the spirit is the innermost man. When
all of these three are fully alive and free of sin, and
functioning in their right relationships to one anoth-

er, you have a human being as God made him to be.

Dr. Andrew Murray, a superlative Bible expositor, wrote that *it is through the spirit that man stands "related to the spiritual world."*

Dr. Murray also penned these telling lines:

"The spirit is the seat of our God-consciousness; the soul of our self-consciousness; the body of our world-conciousness. In the spirit, God dwells; in the soul, self; in the body, sense."

Understand these words and you will be well on your way to an understanding of the nature of man.

In this the writer was speaking of man as he was meant to be, not as he actually is. Self dwells in the soul and sense in the body in every case, but God does not dwell in the spirit of a man in sin. The fact is that evil spirits may dwell in the part of a man meant for the indwelling of God.

We tend to think—I know I did for a long time—of the soul as some extremely vague inner principle—a kind of pale ghost that you can't quite put your finger on. That renders the expression "saving the soul" virtually unintelligible because we don't know what it is that is being saved.

The soul is the human being within the body. It is the you within your body. It is the real you. The self.

Your mind, your will, your emotions, and the ability to express personality are all powers of your soul.

The soul includes the mind and the will of a man. Put another way, it includes all the powers of intellect and volition.

A man's personality and his emotions reside in the soul. It can accurately be said that a man's personality is the expression *of* his soul, but a man's personality is expressed *by* his body.

Genesis 2:7 shows that man had a body, which

God formed out of the dust, before man had life. It was when God "breathed into his nostrils the breath of life" that "man became *a living soul.*"

"A living soul" is what man is essentially. It has been helpfully said that "man *is* a soul, and he *has* a body."

The outward members of your body are instruments you use to carry out the intentions of your soul. If, in an accident, you were to lose a forearm you would not be essentially any less yourself. Your soul would be absolutely intact. It would simply have fewer bodily mechanisms to use, by which to express itself.

Though man is tripartite in his makeup, and though each of these three parts is distinct, man's trinity is fused into a perfect union.

The brain, for example, is the seat of the mind. The brain is part of the body. The mind is a part of the soul.

The mind is certainly greater than the brain. The thoughts that come to us come to our minds. They are received, stored, or dispatched by the brain as instructions to our members. *The brain is the command center of the mind for the body.* The brain relates the mind to the body.

Then there is the human spirit. It is this, above all, that makes man unique. By this part of his being, a man may be in touch with the spiritual realm.

It is the human spirit that gives man his spiritual capacity. It is by this that men may worship God as He desires to be worshiped "in spirit and in truth." Yet this part of man has been ruined by the Fall.

In God's perfect design for man, the human spirit, indwelt and filled by the Holy Spirit and enjoying a full and free communion with the living God, was to govern all the activities and powers of the soul—intellect, will, and emotions. In this plan, man would always act in perfect agreement with the will of his Creator and he would enjoy the fruits of the creation in abundant leisure and in peace.

When man sinned, he was cut off from the life of God. The line was broken between heaven and earth. The communion between the Creator and His creature was gone. The spirit of man became dead toward God—not dead in the sense that it is totally inactive, but in the sense that it is utterly unable to perform its proper function.

Man's spirit, meant to be the dwelling place of God, became at best dead to God and at worst it became an abode of evil spirits. The intention of God was that man, walking in perfect communion and perfect agreement with Him—the human spirit and the Holy Spirit wholly as one—would jointly rule with God outward from the spirit, through the soul and body, to the whole natural environment. Everywhere man went, then, the will of God would be done.

Instead we see another condition entirely. Man, dead in his spirit and lacking communion with God, carries on in the powers of his soul, which inevitably come under some degree of influence by demons (even in the best of men) or, at the worst, he comes under the actual control of evil spirits and therefore spreads chaos and misery in his environment.

It is the spirit of man, not the soul, that God intended to govern his life! The soul is not capable of governing the life aright. With the soul in charge, the center of man's government is misplaced—from God to self.

But it was in their *spirits* that the first humans knew and worshiped God. When they sinned, their spirits became darkened and dead. They no longer had fellowship with God or worshiped Him. They hid from Him.

In doing the will of Satan and cutting himself off from the life of God, however, man did not in any sense cut his spirit off from Satan and the demons. Quite the opposite, man gave access to his spirit to evil spirits. If any man who is, as the Bible puts it, spiritually "dead in trespasses and sins" undertakes to develop his darkened spirit, he does so only by the agency and activity of demonic spirits.

Most Americans are dull, inactive, obtuse in this area of their being. Some are not. There are some who are psychically sensitive, as they say, and full of spiritual perceptions and intuitions of various kinds. They may become highly developed and active in their spirits, but it is all demonic.

Such individuals, who possess certain spiritual capacities or powers, are often not aware of that, since demons usually present themselves and their activities as beneficent, even as Satan "disguises himself as an angel of light" (2 Corinthians, 11:14b, NAS).

Now we see some young people in this nation becoming active in this way. They *know* that there is a spiritual and supernatural realm. They have had experiences in this realm. Some have had encounters with supernatural beings. Whether they know it, or do not know it, these experiences are all demonic in their source.

Man's spirit is dead in trespasses and he therefore cannot have communion with God until his spirit is "made alive by the Spirit of God." The blood of Jesus Christ, shed for human sin, makes this act of regeneration possible.

Such individuals, who truly worship God and know Him, are alive and active in their spirits only because they have been reawakened, made alive in the spirit, born again in the sense of John 3:3.

Their darkened, deadened spirits have been touched by the breath of God—by the Holy Spirit. They are filled with light in the spiritual part and they enjoy daily fellowship with God.

Stages and Degrees of Demonic Control

To the extent that a man becomes involved with demons, to that extent he ceases to be his own master. In the worst cases, a man loses control over certain parts, or over all, of his being. He comes under the power of an alien volition.

There are dramatic instances of this in Scripture and I have seen virtually comparable cases in life. There is the case of the man who came to Jesus and said, " 'Lord have mercy on my son; for he is an epileptic, and is very ill; for he often falls into the fire, and often into the water.' . . . And Jesus rebuked him, and *the demon came out of him,* and the boy was cured at once" (Matthew 17:15, 18, NAS).

It was the alien presence of the demon in the boy that seized him and threw him into the fire or into water and tore him with convulsions. As soon as the demon was cast out of him, the boy came into unchallenged and unbroken control of all his faculties.

You are endowed with certain faculties, and God wants you to enjoy full command and control of those faculties. Satan does not. That is why evil spirits seek to cut in on a man's own power over his actions and thoughts and to take them over by as much as they can.

It may accurately be said that demons work to wreck or damage human beings physically, mentally, morally, emotionally, and spiritually. They have many programs to these ends, and there are many stages, and also many kinds, of demonic activity.

The powers of evil under Satan understand the nature of man quite well. Since man was made in the image of God and was meant to be a perfectly balanced tripartite being—spirit, soul, and body—demons seek to damage or to destroy human beings in those areas.

The demons know the interrelatedness of all the parts of a man's being and if they cannot get a man one way, they are content for the time being to get him in another—knowing that any way they get him will work to the advantage of their over-all program.

Getting a man one way can become the avenue of getting him in other ways later. By goading a man to do what is morally wrong, for instance, demons may adversely affect his emotional or physical well-being.

The Bible speaks of many kinds of evil spirits, identifying them by their varying propensities and by the effects they produce in those they afflict. There are spirits of fear . . . foul spirits . . . spirits of error . . . perverse spirits . . . unclean spirits . . . spirits of jealousy . . . spirits of whoredom . . . lying spirits . . . spirits of infirmity . . . spirits of emulation.

There are also deceiving spirits, sadistic spirits, scheming spirits, spirits of murder, suicide, destruction, violence, accusation, addiction, malice, hatred, and race hatred. There are spirits of divination, and the Bible speaks many times, and always warns against, "familiar spirits." This is but a very partial listing.

The important question is how do demons succeed in putting into practical effect Satan's program for man? There are four major types of sin through which demons gain access to, and a degree of control over, human beings:

Demons gain control through moral sins.

Demons gain control through unbelief.

Demons gain control through false religion or false worship.

Demons gain control through alcohol, narcotics, hallucinogens, or other chemical agents.

Demons gain access and control through *moral sins*—theft, anger, jealousy, lust, or anything else—and if a man's will gives way to a particular sin, *a basis for demonic activity in his life along that line is created.*

Demons gain control through the spiritual sin of *unbelief* because unbelief seeks to ignore or deny the central fact of the universe, that God Is. It is an attempt to obliterate the knowledge and fear of the Creator from His creation. It is the most drastic and elementary and outrageous lie about the nature of the universe. Satan seeks to set up a basis of life that rules God out as totally unnecessary and irrelevant. The Scripture declares that Satan "the god of this world has blinded the minds of them which believe not" so that they remain ignorant of, and indifferent to, God the Creator during their lives (2 Corinthians 4:4a).

An unbeliever's entire life is founded upon a lie, and everything that he does, whether apparently good or bad proceeds out of that lie. The Scripture therefore says that "what is not of faith is sin" (Romans 14:23a).

Demons gain control through false religions and false worship of every kind because these sins are the most express contradiction of the will of God, that He alone be worshiped and that His truth be believed. Satan stands behind every form of religion not revealed by God, and many of the practices of such religions are specifically demonic. They are all designed to lead men into spiritual bondage or keep them in it, and there is no liberating power in them. They are set up to give demons sway over men and they prevent men from finding reconciliation to God.

From Temptation to Possession

It is an almost inevitable rule of sin that it pays off at a steadily diminishing rate, so that you have to have more and more of it to get the same result as time goes on. In the same process, its pains and sorrows steadily increase.

Temptation is the most common work of evil spirits and, as it proves effective, it may be succeeded by the more severe stages of demonic activity aimed at individual men—*oppression, obsession and possession.*

No sharp line can be drawn between demon oppression and obsession. Obsession is oppression amplified and intensified. Demon oppression may take many different forms; it is usually experienced in the moods, in the feelings, in the emotional state, and also in the mind. The same is true of obsession; the difference is in degree. Oppression may be cyclic; obsession bears down hard and knows little, if any, relief.

Oppression may come in the form of various moods, perhaps a spell of gloom or melancholy that may come suddenly or without apparent reason. This occupies the seat of a person's emotions and to some extent it governs his actions, perceptions and responses. Human beings were never intended to be ruled or run by transient emotions and moods, but that has become a part of their victimization.

Fear is very often directly produced by the activity of demons and it should be resisted. There can be vague, almost nameless, fears, and there can be knife-sharp, highly distressing fears. They are meant to reduce human efficiency by setting up barriers (unseen but no less formidable) to full, free activity. Fears have a tremendous inhibiting power. When fear seizes a person it can stop him dead from doing what he needs to do or ought to do, and what he would surely do if fear was not there.

Perhaps the most extreme form of inhibiting fear is expressed in the life of the recluse. Some years ago the Collier brothers set up thick barriers of newspaper piles inside their town house in Manhattan and left only tunnel-like passages through the piles, to keep them safe from the outside world and intruders. One of the brothers exited and entered through the passages only for food. They withdrew from all participation in society and normal life, obsessed by fears.

While crawling through a passage, one of the brothers tripped a trap, bringing piles of newspapers down on him. Since he could not move, he died there in his own trap. Deep inside the house, the other man slowly starved to death. The thing intended by them, in their obsession, to be the means of protection became the means of death. They were betrayed by acting according to their fears.

Some individuals who are afflicted with demons must engage in many of their waking hours in a painful and very difficult struggle for the free and efficient use of their faculties, and often they must somehow limp along with only half, or less than half, of the full use of some parts of their being.

Demons can and do attack human beings in their nerves and their muscular systems, as well as in their minds. Sudden experiences of acute nervousness, unexplained by any immediate or outward circumstances, can be caused by direct demonic attacks. If this proceeds far enough, it can ultimately lead to nervous collapse.

I was sent to cover a hippie event—mainly an electronic rock concert—on the Mall in Central Park one summer day, and there I talked with a tall young man, pleasant-looking and entirely pleasant in demeanor and also obviously intelligent, wearing a kind of gypsy clothes and beads. The most obvious thing about him was that he was extremely nervous. This showed in a quavering of his voice and in the shaking of his hands. He had probably got into some demonic realm in his hippie life and he was already paying a price in high nervousness and tension.

There is a more extreme form of demon control. It is the full, acute seizure, in which evil spirits convulse or throw the body of the man they occupy, or make him do bodily harm to himself or attack others—well illustrated in the case of Gottliebin Dittus, discussed in chapter one.

Seizure is a very good word. It is the seizing of control of a person's muscular and nervous systems from him by another force and employing them against him, against his will.

I was riding on a bus in upstate New York one afternoon when a woman about 28 years old got on and sat three rows in front of me. About once every 40 or 50 seconds a shudder passed through her shoulders, her head would jerk, and she barked once or twice like a dog. In every other way her behavior and movements were ordinary and apparently normal. She was a victim of brief, regular seizures, which must have made her life one of indescribable misery.

The uttering of animal sounds involuntarily is a recurrent phenomenon among some persons under demon control. At one of the big pop-rock summer festivals a group of young people had a barking session.

The demonic action opposite to convulsions is that in which the evil spirits freeze human faculties, so to speak, rendering them immobile so that a person cannot use them freely. This is best described as binding a person.

On one occasion, Jesus said, " 'You dumb and deaf spirit, I charge you, come out of him, and never enter him again.' And the spirit cried out and convulsed him terribly, and came out . . ." (Mark 9:25b, 26). The same demon produced two extreme, but opposite, effects. It had the power to block hearing and speaking in the victim, but just as the demon was to be cast out, it cried out aloud through the victim and convulsed him. When the demon came out, the boy could hear and speak clearly and soon he was in full motor control of his body.

In some forms, binding takes the mode of a deformity of posture. There is a man who regularly passes through my New York neighborhood who is terribly bent over and whose right shoulder is thrust up abnormally high. To look up he has to turn his whole face sidewise, and you see one eye cocked upward. He is extremely religious and will not cross a street without making the sign of the cross several times. His religious fixation is as demonic as his deformity undoubtedly is. He is bound in body and bound in spirit.

The Bible says that Jesus was "teaching in one of the synagogues on the Sabbath. And behold, there was a woman who for 18 years had had a *sickness caused by a spirit;* and she was bent double, and could not straighten up at all. And when Jesus saw her, He called her over and said to her, 'Woman, you are freed from your sickness.' To the synagogue

ruler who rebuked Him for healing on the Sabbath,
Jesus replied, "And this woman, a daughter of
Abraham as she is, whom Satan has bound for 18
long years, should she not have been released from
this bond on the Sabbath day?" (Luke 13:10-16,
NAS).

Entire Possession

Evil spirits may affect, or control, a man's
thoughts, his actions, his beliefs, his health, his feelings, his speech, his drives, his passions, or any
other critical sector of his life and being.

*A man who is possessed by a demon or by de-
mons does not have control of himself in the area in
which he is possessed.*

A man who is demon-*possessed* does not do the
will of God, he does not even do his own will. He
does the will of Satan. For more than 15 years a
short, raggedly dressed woman in late middle age
with iron-gray hair, walked up and down the streets
of my neighborhood nearly every afternoon and
evening, shouting angrily in rapid-fire, staccato
bursts. She used a rolled-up newspaper as her
megaphone. There was an electric quality to her
speech, and most of it was in garbled words.

She was not doing her own will; she was fully
possessed and was driven daily, for years, to spend
herself on the sidewalks in such futile actions.

One night I was out with a group of college students and ministers, speaking from a portable pulpit to a small group of people. A man about 25
years old came along, stopped, got down on his
back in front of our pulpit and lay flat, and began
screaming. After a while, he sat cross-legged and
made loud noises. Then he got up and did a kind of
dance. Finally, he tried to stand on the pulpit. It

was an extraordinary performance until it was interrupted by a policeman who came by and took him around the corner. We then continued, after 10 minutes of the most absurd and strenuous interruptions. The mere fact that the words of the Scripture were being spoken publicly at that place had turned this passerby on, so to speak, or had turned the demons in him on and made them put him through a series of wild gyrations designed to drown out what we were saying and seize the public attention. Much of the content of what he shouted, it should be noted, had to do with a Far Eastern religion.

There are many degrees of demonic interference with the use of human faculties—from occasional and partial all the way to total. Just as physical paralysis can be anywhere from partial to total—from a hand up to the entire body, involving one part, several parts, or the whole—so it is with evil spirits.

A person may have one evil spirit who possesses him in one area of his being. He may have a number of evil spirits who possess him in that area or in more than one area of his being. Or he may have many evil spirits who effectively possess him entirely. Mary Magdalene, to whom Jesus appeared first after His resurrection, is described as a woman "out of whom He had cast seven devils" (literally, "demons"; Mark 16:9; Luke 8:2). When Jesus asked the man in the tombs his name, he said, "My name is Legion, for we are many."

So evil spirits may possess a man in some, several, or all aspects of his being, and in those areas he is overmastered by them and does their will.

Chapter 10

Satan's Three-Part
Program for Young People

If you were to make a survey of a hundred American adults over 35 and were to ask them if they believed in the activity of supernatural spirits, a heavy majority would say no. If you put the same question to a hundred Americans between 17 and 24 years old, a majority would probably say yes—and that is a big clue to the generation gap. The older people mainly think there is no such activity. Many of the younger people *know* there is.

We are going to find the key to what is happening to so many young people in this area, and if we do not face that fact, we are not going to be able to meet the difficulties into which they are so rapidly falling. Nor are they.

While with one hand Satan has in a large degree taken away the truth of God and the joys of true supernatural experience from this generation, he has with the other hand brought upon it a vast new traffic in false mysticism and contact with evil spirits.

A few weeks ago I was visiting the offices of a company where I have some friends. I had come to know a number of persons there. But I had not met the young Jew (23 years old) in the following brief account, though I had seen him in the place. It was 5:30 P.M. and I was about to leave when a friend said, "Wait. Leonard Marks [not his real name] is sitting in the back corner. He's crying. There's something wrong and he says he wants to talk to you."

"Who is Leonard Marks?" I asked.

"You'll recognize him," he said. "Just go back and talk to him. Maybe you can help him. He had a nervous breakdown a few months ago."

That part of the office had closed for the night and it was dark there. I walked back and found the young man sitting on top of a desk, with tears in his eyes. I recognized him as a bright, vividly alert, energetic young man who had been working as an assistant to several executives.

"What's wrong?" I asked.

What came in answer didn't make sense. "I want to be the flag-bearer on the new Cobra helicopter," he said. "The Cobra is different. It's going to be a force for good. I'm a member of the new generation, and I want to be the flag-bearer on it."

I tried to get him to explain what being the flag-bearer would be, but he said he was a member of the new generation. "I have ideas, new generation ideas, that this company needs," he said. "I want power here." A moment later he talked about becoming "President of the United States." Then he described himself as "a member of the Mod Squad."

"Why did you ask me to come back here to see you?" I asked.

"You know about the supernatural," he said.

"Yes," I said. I talked to him directly and quietly: "Leonard, this thing that's got hold of you is out to destroy you."

His head fell. "Yes, I know that," he said.

I knew that something had pulled him off the track and I began to have an idea what it was. "What have you been taking?" I asked.

"I took marijuana on Saturday night," he said. "I haven't taken any LSD. I've had marijuana a few times."

He said he did not intend to take LSD and that he thought he would not take any more marijuana because—and this is especially significant—he now believed it was possible for him "to experience the supernatural without marijuana."

The other side of that, obviously, is that *he had experienced the supernatural by taking marijuana.*

Then he left that theme and began to tell me how he had found it possible to seduce almost any girl by a whirlwind campaign including great personal attention, kindness, carefully selected gifts (ascertaining what she liked and then going to any length to find exactly that thing), doing together the things she liked best to do. The technique was to show every outward evidence of a genuine affection, having in mind, however, the single object of seduction at each step.

He talked about meditation next. He said that he had taken up the practice at home of just sitting, gurulike, and letting his mind wander in daydreams, fantasies. He had read *The Prophet*, he said, and several books on mysticism, psychic phenomena, yoga.

Later one of the executives told me that everybody liked Leonard, that he had always been a good, quick worker, but that lately he had "gone off on a lot of grandiose ideas." He had taken a memorandum written by one of the executives, revised it, and told a secretary to have it mimeographed and distributed in his new form.

"When did all this begin with you, Leonard? All this meditation and psychic stuff?" I asked.

"It started about a year ago when I watched the Maharishi Yogi on television one night. He was laughing and giggling a lot and, I mean, there was something wrong with him," he said.

"What was the next step?"

"Yoga, mind over matter, psychic energy, books. I sat on the edge of my bed at home, daydreaming, and I got all these great ideas. Listen, if I could put some of them into action it would really be great. I have an idea for a new way of running this company. . . ."

I warned him that if he did not get back to reality he could lose his mind. For almost four years he had been able to hold a good job in an executive office of the company, but then suddenly his behavior and speech had become strangely erratic. The process that threatened his stability was not hard to trace. He happened to see a guru on television. That got him interested in meditation, yoga, the occult, psychic phenomena, and he went out and bought books on these things—nearly every book rack has them—and began to read heavily in these areas. He took marijuana several times.

Because he is a Jew, the shock effect of these forces hit him faster and harder than they would have hit a Gentile—for reasons I shall go into later. Under the suasions of the demon religions of the East he had suffered two nervous breakdowns in a year. A few weeks later he lost his job.

Notice three specific things in the life of Leonard Marks which, in his early twenties, had carried him to this point:

First, involvement with the mysticism of the East.

Second, taking marijuana.

Third, the sin of fornication.

There you have it: *Fornication . . . marijuana . . . mysticism . . .* the three-part program of Satan for the young people of this nation today, and he is pushing it from every side in a highly concentrated attack. It is this demonic program whose effects are felt at high school and college campuses all over the nation. And it is this program whose effects on teenagers and young adults have made them susceptible to violence and disorder.

You cannot go onto the major college campuses without being made aware of this three-pronged push. It is in the campus papers, on posters, in leaflets, in discussion groups, in magazines aimed at young people, in the bookstores, in the demands of student rebels, in the air. And, of course, much of it is also in that favorite medium of the young, the motion pictures.

Each of these three things can open an avenue for demons into the inner being of a young person. All three together provide a basis for a crashing influx of evil spirits, full of potent disintegrative effects.

I use the term marijuana to cover what is broadly called "the drug scene." The big push for marijuana began about 1966, as did the push for the stronger hallucinogens, such as LSD.

On its heels came the big push for "the wisdom of the East," for "transcendental meditation," for gurus and Eastern mysticism and Hinduism, for the paraphernalia of idolatry and the supernaturalism that goes with it. By 1969, cruder forms of demonic supernaturalism—occultism and witchcraft—were coming conspicuously on the scene.

The big push for the throwing down of parietal rules inhibiting social, and especially sexual, communication between young men and women in college gained considerable momentum in 1967 and 1968.

Anything that increases the possibilities of, and the temptations to, fornication fits into Satan's purposes perfectly, and he supports it with all the zeal and skill of his genius for promotion (advancing apologies and encouragements, contrary to the Word of God, from all kinds of supposedly expert sources) because this sin is useful to him in destroying human beings.

The tempter knows that if he can get young people to give themselves over briefly to the electric pleasure to be had in an illicit act of fornication, he has a chance of producing a harvest of suffering out of it—a time of shame and fear for a pregnant girl and years of unshared burden in raising a not-really-wanted child; a sense of guilt for the young man; a dangerous operation perhaps; a suicide possibly; a marriage of necessity that will link for years or for life two persons not suited to each other; above all, a chance at bringing misery or unwantedness or perversion into the life of the child. The consequences, which run on for years, sometimes for generations, are not in any way worth the flashing pleasures of a moment.

Even in those cases where there are no manifest physical or social consequences there are *spiritual consequences to such an act*. "Flee fornication," the Bible says. "Every sin that a man does is without the body, but he that commits fornication sins against his own body" (1 Corinthians 6:18).

God's blessing rests upon true marriage, but His curse falls upon fornication, and those who engage in it suffer effects in some way. Because He loves man, God shows the thing in its true light. Satan always puts *all* the emphasis on the short-term pleasures. He seeks to publicize and glamorize and emphasize the pleasure, and to deny or conceal or mock the payoff. "It will not be so in your case," he suggests. "You will escape." The Scripture says, "Be sure your sin will find you out." The Book of The

Revelation solemnly declares that "murderers, fornicators, sorcerers, idolators, and all liars—their lot shall be in the lake of fire that burns" forever (21:8).

A man's sin will find him out at some future, inconvenient time. Whether soon or late, it will track him down. Tens of thousands of young women have gone through long, drab years of loneliness and suffering because on one evening years before they agreed to break a law of God.

Any one of these three things—premarital or nonmarital sex, Eastern mysticism, and marijuana or LSD—supplies a basis for direct demonic activity in the lives of those who indulge in them. Combined, they provide the basis for a massive invasion of demonic spirits. Thus students are softened up for the push for anarchism, rebellion, insurgency.

As these three things also reach down into the high schools and the junior high schools, similar conditions of disruption and destructiveness will break out there, as they have begun to do. It is the tragic result of the increasing degree of influence and control that demons have gained in the lives of young people through sin.

The Origin of the Youth Subculture

There has been created in the United States a youth culture, or subculture, that is distinct from the national culture. It has sprung up, in part, as a revolt against a national culture that has become fat and sleek and in some ways swinish. Yet the fact that the youth culture rejects many evils of the adult culture does not make the youth culture itself exempt from evil.

There are elements in it that are identifiably demonic and that incite the young into doing things directly contrary to God's commandments.

The present youth subculture, as a phenomenon apart from the larger culture in which it is an island, is a product of the 1960s. It did not take shape all at once; it came by stages. It is interesting to see where it came from.

If there is a single chief, *outward* identifying mark of the many-pronged demonic attack on the stability and well-being of young people today it is hair grown long or wild. It is part of the uniform of youth's great restlessness.

That particular manifestation of youth's desire to be at obvious variance with those who are older started with four young men from Liverpool, England—the Beatles quartet. Long hair was their trademark. As they were lifted up into international celebrity and made known to just about every teenager in the English-speaking nations and in Europe, their copious hair was constantly displayed in photographs. The long-hair style flooded in upon the youth through the Beatles' example.

There was apparently no intention other than to have a distinctive trademark as a means of special identification and promotion, but it set the trend among many young people. (See 1 Corinthians 11:14.)

The Beatles, as exemplars, did not stop at hair and hard rock. As trend-setters for youth they were used, at just the critical moment, to open a wedge into the West for the religious mysticism of the East.

It was their act, as they stood at the absolute height of their fame among the young, of seeking out the Maharishi Yogi for spiritual counsel that, more than any single factor, raised him to renown in the West. Mia Farrow, the actress, reinforced the Indian mystic's vogue a few weeks later, in October 1967, when she went to his Himalayan retreat in search of "a higher spiritual experience." The preceding August the Beatles had sought the Yogi out. A news report quoted the Yogi as saying, "They came backstage after one of my lectures, and they said to me, 'Even from an early age we have been seeking a highly spiritual experience. We tried drugs and that didn't work.'"

All the publicity and photographs that flowed from these encounters brought the Yogi and his concept of transcendental meditation to mass attention in the United States, so that the Beatles became *spiritually instrumental* among the young.

One of the Beatles made a gratuitous, but quite accurate, remark that the quartet was more popular than Jesus Christ. It is not the factualness of the remark that is significant; it is the thrust and inference of it.

The quartet became immensely influential among young people in half the world.

The Beatles were just one of a great many teen-age quartets working in relative obscurity, until they were discovered, altered, and then promoted into a world craze by a young man named Brian Epstein.

Brian Epstein, mastermind of the staggering phenomenon that was known as Beatlemania, first encountered them in 1961 as "four scruffy lads in leather jackets and jeans who hung around the [Epstein family's record] store in the afternoons." He made himself their manager and business agent.

I interviewed Brian Epstein during the Beatles' first visit to New York City. I met him at the Plaza, where I found him settled in as plush and spacious a suite as I have ever seen (and I have seen the one the President stays in at the Waldorf-Astoria), a young man sitting on top of the world and quite aware of it. He was making money at an astonishing rate, had scores more booking invitations than he could possibly fulfill, and at that time he controlled by far the hottest property in show business.

For the five young men at the heart of this operation, the quartet and their manager, there came wealth and success in heaping measures. Brian Epstein was a multimillionaire at thirty and he had made the four others millionaires, too. *Newsweek* said that Mr. Epstein led "a revolution in popular music that changed the sensibility of a generation and made John, Paul, Ringo, and George worldwide icons." That is influence!

Brian Epstein was found dead in bed at his home in Chapel Street on August 27, 1967. "He had earned $14 million in five years," the *London Times* reported, in his dizzying projection of the quartet. And, as the paper said, "he had made five LSD trips in one fourteen-month period." Certainly Brian Epstein was socially and culturally influential on a large scale in the West, yet he became a victim of the very subculture he did so much to form.

Here is the lead of a *London Times* dispatch:

"Mr. Brian Epstein, aged 32, manager of the Beatles, was killed by the cumulative effect of a bromide in a drug he had been taking for some time, a Westminster inquest was told yesterday. The coroner, Mr. Gavin Thruston, said death was due to poisoning by Carbrital, due to an incautious self-overdose. He said Mr. Epstein had been taking sleeping tablets for a long time and had 'perpetual trouble with insomnia.' The coroner had 'found a trace of an anti-depressant drug, and barbiturate and bromide' in the body."

Mr. Epstein had discovered them and brought them to their amazing pinnacle, but the quartet had wearied of him. *Time* magazine sounded this melancholy note: "When Epstein died last week, the

Beatles were some 225 miles away in Wales getting initiated into an Indian mystic cult led by Maharishi Yogi." At Brian's funeral service in a Liverpool synagogue, the magazine noted, "no Beatle was present."

In the wild race that led him finally to insomnia and barbiturates and anti-depressants and LSD and death, young Mr. Epstein probably sought nothing more complicated than fame, success, money, and he got them all by heaps. Yet in making those his ends, he served other causes.

Fame, success, money proved enough to bribe his soul to spend himself and all his energies and genius in the promotion of that meteoric and dazzling, if historically momentary, craze called Beatlemania. In its hour there was nothing quite like it in the Western world—it was certainly "more popular than Jesus"—and its grip on the youth was tremendous. The impact of Brian Epstein's influence fell upon millions of young people and it fell upon them in a way that exploited them, in a way that stirred them to adulation and imitation and frenzy. It was just a trademark that the Beatles wore their hair that way. It was just an oddity that an entire Beatles performance would be drowned out by a chorus of young voices raised in one continuous, high-pitched shriek. The Beatles gave them the big beat—in music and in emotions. Out of it all, that whole vapid, frenzied, tumultuous mania, there began to emerge certain patterns among the young —a style of dress, an urge toward a kind of animalism, a low running fever of rebellion against adult-sanctioned authority, a drop-out psychology, a studied neglect of standards of civilized usage, a search for immediate and short-term sensations in sex and pot and "mind-expansion" agents and, later, a quest into the mystery religions of the East. These patterns soon became a culture apart. The Beatles were not responsible for it all by any means, but they began it, set some of its most obtrusive styles, rode it like a wild steed; and the Beatles made the big breakthrough into the West for yogism and Eastern mysticism. Altogether, it was a trend-setting of potent impact on the young.

For a time the message that millions of the young were getting was the Beatles' message—in music, in manner, in lyrics, in dress. That message has since flowered into a rock culture full of mystical dreamscapes and picturesque unreality, of psychedelia, of life lived in brief interludes of pulsing tempo and driving excitation on the electronic upbeat, the sex upbeat, the narcotics upbeat, the "speed" upbeat, succeeded by longer interludes of listlessness, hopelessness, apathy, lethargy—alternating cycles of stimulation and depression. A major part of the program is to get young people out of reality, and the ability to cope with reality, into unreality and disinclination to become meaningfully or constructively engaged with their environment. The step beyond that is to get them destructively engaged with their environment.

The Beatles set the trends, but they have since been replaced by scores of groups of similar or imitative mode, some of appalling depravity that have sunk much lower, and are far more gross in their expressions of animality, groups which are plugging Satan's message in the most explicit way.

In merely failing to serve God and in serving himself, Brian Epstein fell unwittingly into the service of Satan. A person does not have to serve demons knowingly to serve their cause; he only has to serve *wrong ends*. When a man makes his ultimate goal that which is neither ultimate nor of any true worth, and consecrates all the energies and powers of his soul to it, the demons appropriate it to Satan's cause.

When Epstein found them, the Beatles were earning $10.50 a night. "One did everything," he told me. "One shouted from the rooftops . . . People thought you were mad, but you went on shouting."

Brian Epstein found a cause, but it is not the cause to which the Jews are called.

Because he meant them to be the channels of godliness to all mankind, God has put into the Jews a disproportionately high capacity to be influential in society. They have used this to many ends—some of them humanly very good, some highly destructive (consider the immense effect of Karl Marx on history in loosing the false religion of Communism on mankind)—but rarely to the purpose for which it is designed: "And now, Israel, what does the Lord your God require of you, but to fear the Lord your God, to walk in all His ways, to love Him, and to serve the Lord your God with all your heart and all your soul" (Deuteronomy 10:12).

When a man puts God first in his life, the wisdom and order of God come into that life and set it in a vast harmony with all the purposes of God in the universe. It brings him into line with God's whole order of things.

Brian Epstein became, in a sense, the father of a generation. He undoubtedly possessed a huge capacity for public influence. He exercised it to immeasurable effect, yet never to any godly purpose. He got the kind of package the devil loves to give: fast, short-term thrills and rewards, with enough poison thrown in to send him down into the grave at 32. He served the devil's purposes and he got the devil's deal.

When we put our faculties out to lesser purposes than those for which they were designed, we deny them to God and we put them at the disposal of Satan. A person may be more guilty of that than he knows, because he cannot see the whole effect of what he does. Millions of humans do the devil's work without having any idea that they do it.

We selfishly reserve ourselves for ourselves and seek our own good, and by doing that we fall into his service. It is not done by intention, but by omission—but such an omission! To omit God in our lives, in our plans, in our pursuits is to omit our Creator, the giver of every good and every perfect gift, and to admit Satan. Why? Because self-service is Satan's first principle: I WILL make my plans, I WILL choose my goals, I WILL run my own life—it is all the echo of Satan's drastic rebellion against God, his adamant refusal to let God be God to him.

The world would have said, looking at the achievements of Brian Epstein, that he was serving his own ends and doing a terrific job of it, piling up the millions for a future that, as it turned out, he did not have.

I said earlier that the fact that the young man I called Leonard Marks is a Jew, rather than a Gentile, had caused his deterioration under the impact of sexual sin, Eastern mysticism, and marijuana to proceed more rapidly. Let me explain that now.

Such things are dangerous for anybody who goes into them, but they are emphatically more so for a Jew than for a Gentile. A Gentile is born and lives under no special obligation toward God arising from his origin, his forebears, or his race.

A Jew is born under a special calling of God. The purpose of God in calling Abraham was to establish a separate people through whom He would start to drive back the influence and works of Satan in the earth and begin to increase His influence and works among mankind. Through Abraham and his descendants (the Jews), God promised that "all the families of the earth shall be blessed" (Genesis 12:3).

If the Jews had lent themselves unreservedly to that purpose, what benefits the earth would have received by it!

God commanded the Jews to be absolutely different from Gentiles in regard to false worship, to idols, and to sin. David of Israel declared, "I love Thy commandments above gold; yes, above fine gold. Therefore I esteem all thy precepts concerning all things to be right, and I hate every false way" (Psalm 119:127, 128).

A blessing comes upon every Jew who discovers his true spiritual identity. The blessing was promised by God through Moses, but Moses also pronounced a curse upon Jews who forsake the distinctive spiritual obligations that Jewishness places upon them. "Behold, I set before you this day a blessing and a curse," he said. "A blessing, if you obey . . . a curse, if you will not obey" (Deuteronomy 11:26-28).

A blessing is the active favor of God upon an individual, a family, or a nation. A curse is the active disfavor of God upon an individual, a family, or a nation.

The rules are not the same for the Jews. God has given special rules, and special privileges to the Jews, and they wield special influence among the masses of mankind. When they turn their singular capacities and gifts to purposes directly contrary to the will of God, they walk head-on into trouble.

"That is not fair," comes the objection. But it is fair. It is preeminently fair that God has called one people in the world to be His, intending to show His goodness and His power to all mankind through them. What is not fair, to God or to mankind, is that Jews have refused for the most part to allow God to use them in that way, and they have instead run after the follies and excesses of the Gentiles. They have too often demonstrated the curse instead of the blessing.

Something More Than a Beat

There is something more to rock and roll than just music throbbing in the air. Some of it has spiritual dynamism, and some of it is a throwback to tribal ritual. You can "groove" on it. Go into any of the dark areas of the world, where demonic religions hold sway, and you will find tribes whose members at times dance themselves into frenzy to the vibrations of loud, drumming music. Such music sometimes has an evil energy that produces violence.

This is not a blanket condemnation of the rock idiom; it is not all of a piece. However, it should be recognized that there are spiritual effects attending the use of some of it. Consider a paragraph from a story about the religious use of rock music that ran in the *Times*:

" 'The music lets your consciousness expand,' said Joe Frazier, a student at the Berkeley Divinity School in New Haven whose group, the Eschaton, performed at the Yale service. 'It brings out a sense of community and *some fantastic commerce with the spirit and the soul.*' "

That is exactly so. Evil spirits produce such effects in the human soul and spirit through the impulses and vibrations of such music, and some of this music involves a commerce with evil spirits. That is why rock concerts of the more frenzied kind have sometimes been immediately followed by outbreaks of violence. Spiritually, that kind of rock music is an emergence of tribalism in this country.

Chapter 11

Drugs
and the Supernatural

There is a direct and mysterious relationship between certain chemical agents and the supernatural. Certain drugs can carry the user into the realm of the demons. By taking these agents into his body a person opens up avenues into his soul and spirit by which evil spirits may enter and seize a measure of control. He also opens his body, particularly his nerves and muscular system, to demonic interference and physical damage.

As a previous chapter has set forth, God wants man to be in full command and control of his faculties. Satan wants to rob man of the full use and control of his faculties, and alcohol, narcotics, and hallucinogens are potent elements for cutting in on a man's own control of his mind and body. He therefore widely promotes their use among populations of the world.

There is a certain class of chemicals and drugs that grow on the earth that have profound effects on the human system when they are taken into it. I call them chemical-supernatural agents because these drugs can, and frequently do, introduce people to the supernatural. Certain drugs provide a shortcut to the supernatural.

That is no secret; it is an advertised and well known facet of the narcotics experience. Men such as William James, Havelock Ellis, Aldous Huxley, and Timothy Leary have written of the spiritual and supernatural aspects of drug use. James, who is said to have used nitrous oxide as an hallucinogenic agent, wrote of "other forms of consciousness" and stressed that the existence of these forms "forbid a premature closing of our accounts with reality." That, essentially, was what Leary was talking about when he spoke of "consciousness expansion." It is contended that an introduction to these other forms of consciousness, as they are called, is good, broadening, beneficial, liberating. A closer look will show that it is quite exactly the opposite of these.

The use of certain chemical agents as spiritual agents (expressly in order to be put into contact with the supernatural) is a deeply entrenched practice in certain parts of the world, usually among people of low achievement, slack culture, and little or no education.

Peyote is distinctively used in religious ceremonies and rituals. It is among the best known of the natural hallucinogens. In some places it is used by people desiring to enter into a visionary state.

"Visions and other mystical experiences are part of the regular spiritual diet of the 50,000-odd members of the Native American Church, thanks to what they consider a special gift from God: peyote, a small cactus growing in the valley of the Rio Grande," one report on the plant said. "The Indians of the Native American Church cut off and dry the cactus tops, then eat the 'buttons' in night-long ceremonies to the accompaniment of sacred fire and chanting.

"The faith's adherents believe that the partaking of peyote brings one into direct contact with God. They also address prayers to it, and consider it to be a protector."

There is, of course, no plant or drug that can put a man "into direct contact with God." The living God does not reveal Himself to a man on the basis of his taking a chemical into his system. Peyote can, however, open up an avenue of contact with an unseen spirit.

The United States had been almost entirely free of this tandem of Satanic evil until relatively recent years.

A man who did much to introduce the spiritual applications in the use of certain drugs to the American consciousness is R. Gordon Wasson, a New York banker and a mycologist of recognized distinction. He credits himself with "the rediscovery of the religious role of the hallucinogenic mushrooms of Mexico." He and his wife spent part of 1955 among native cultists there.

"When we first went down to Mexico, we felt certain, my wife and I, that we were on the trail of an ancient and holy mystery, and we went as pilgrims seeking the Grail," he said in a lecture in 1960. An ancient mystery, yes—but not a holy one. It is filled with cultic practices repugnant to the Scriptures and specifically enjoined by them.

The Wassons became probably "the first outsiders . . . to be invited to partake in the *agape* of the sacred mushroom." They found that "this middle-American cult of a divine mushroom, this cult of 'God's flesh' as the Indians in pre-Columbian times called it, can be traced back to about 1500 B.C. . . . Thus we find a mushroom in the center of the cult with perhaps the oldest continuous history in the world."

Mr. Wasson presented this rite of the demons to the United States in 1957 when *Life* opened its pages to a major article by him called "Seeking the Magic Mushroom." Theodore Roszak later noted that this "splashy and appetizing feature," which provided "detailed illustrations and descriptions of the mushrooms, made all the familiar connections with occult and Oriental religions."

Mr. Wasson, banker and mushroom pilgrim, notes that the mushroom enables a man "to travel backwards and forwards in time, to enter other planes of existence, even [as the Indians say] to know God."

Or, as the Greek scholar Mary Barnard wrote in *The American Scholar,* concerning a dozen plants used in religious practices, "Some of them are open doors to the otherworld. . . . They are sacred plants, magic herbs or shrubs . . . magic carpets on which the spirit of the shaman can travel through time and space. . . . The magic plants are vehicles for a special kind of experience adaptable to the use of most religions that acknowledge an otherworld and permit its exploration."

A classic myth suggests that the use of these plants for supernatural purposes came by direct demonic revelation. Miss Barnard writes that "The peyote myth tells how an Indian, or several Indians, . . . is lost or wounded and left for dead in an uninhabited desert region. Starving, thirsty, at the end of his strength, he stumbles upon the peyote. A voice tells him to eat it. He eats it and feels his strength miraculously restored. His hunger and thirst are alleviated, and he is able to make his way back to his people, to whom he bears the word of a new god sent to heal their suffering. Usually the Indian hears a voice directing him to eat the plant, or sees a godlike form in the shape of an Indian brave standing where the plant stood; in some versions he is given instructions by Peyote himself on the proper performance of the peyote ritual."

One thing that may be said of any such revelation

as that is that it is not of God, but that it *is* demonic. The voice, the vision, and the revelation of the supernatural uses of the drug plant all fall into the category of the activity of evil spirits. Their function is to deceive men, especially to deceive them spiritually.

Ellis wrote of "the artificial paradise of mescal" (peyote), but that is not quite what it is. It is a counterfeit paradise and that paradise can turn in an instant into a living hell.

Evil spirits, posing as gods, gain entrance to human beings and control them when humans use such substances.

"The sacred mushrooms of Oaxaca are taken raw, on an empty stomach, like the fresh peyote," Miss Barnard writes. "When the shaman has swallowed the mushroom, the mushroom-deity takes possession of the shaman's body and speaks with the shaman's lips. The shaman does not say whether the sick child will live or die; *the mushroom says.* Some Indians say of sacred plants used by their shaman, that the soul of an ancestor has entered the plant; it is he who takes possession of the shaman and speaks through his mouth." This is none other than possession of the body by evil spirits and their use of the faculties of the one they possess.

In a review called "The Magic of Peyote," Dudley Young discussed a book called *The Teachings of Don Juan* by Carlos Castaneda, giving a glimpse into the nightmare experiences that an individual can suffer through involvement with drug plants, especially through a religious involvement. He wrote:

"This book is the record of a young anthropologist's experiences as the apprentice of a Mexican Indian sorcerer. Over a period of four years, Mr. Castaneda paid intermittent visits to Don Juan, first in Arizona, then in Sonora, Mexico. The aim of his initiation was to gain power over the demonic world through the ritualized ingestion of peyote and other hallucinogenic plants." What happened, however, was that the demons began to gain power over Mr. Castaneda. Mr. Young goes on: "Mr. Castaneda's descriptions of his experiences with peyote are both interesting and moving. It made him violently ill and disclosed to him both terror and ecstasy. Towards the end of his fourth year he began to have what the layman might describe as a nervous breakdown, and after a particularly shattering evening with the Don, he abruptly broke off relations.

"Don Juan emerges as an enigmatic, ultimately sinister *guru* figure; ascetic and authoritarian."

Mr. Young says that it was not clear whether Don Juan was "seeking a corrupting kind of power over his disciple," but "Certainly the author's final hallucination, during which he threw a rock at his master who seemed bent on destroying him, would support such a suggestion."

Mr. Castaneda apparently broke with his whole misadventure at just the point at which the takeover was about to be completed, and it is a significant sign of the sharpness of his resistance that he threw a rock at the sorcerer leading him on.

There have been repeated reports of sex crimes, often against children, committed under the influence of peyote. Peyote is not a blessed substance; it is a cursed substance. It can damage men physically, mentally, spiritually.

Drugs are a means by which Satan can take you out of your own control and begin to bring you under his control. He wants to take controls at the center of your being and make them subject to his spiritual agents, demons. Drug experiences can be the beginning of the seizing of a person's mind and will, a means of carrying him into regions of fantasy, euphoria, terror, passivity, anomie, apathy, lethargy, distorted perspective, mental and spiritual confusion, false worship, insanity.

That would not be terribly important if chemical-supernatural agents were not being widely popularized in the United States. Timothy Leary did much to lead the way as an early "promoter, apologist, and high priest of dope," the mass evangelist of "instant mysticism." It is significant that when Leary formulated his passion for drug-induced experiences into a cult, he called it the League for Spiritual Discovery—LSD. He announced in 1966 that he was founding a "new" religion based on the sacramental use of LSD, peyote, and marijuana.

The Bible warns men against "giving heed to seducing spirits and doctrines of demons" (1 Timothy 4:1b).

There is a curse that lies upon the earth, and there are things that grow in the earth upon which Satan has made a claim. These plants are inimical to the welfare and health of human beings in a mysteriously numerous variety of ways. The same plant may affect one person one way, another person another way, a third another way, and many other people in many other ways, each different yet all deleterious to well-being.

Before man did the bidding of Satan and, by it, entered into sin, there was nothing in the whole realm of nature on earth that was bad for or harmful to man.

When God told man of the consequences of the sin of disobedience, one of the things God said was, *"Cursed is the ground* because of you. . . ." Among the effects of that curse was that "thorns and thistles it shall grow for you" (Genesis 3:17, 18, NAS).

There had never been any such things in the

ground, but now there came out of the ground new and strange plants bearing thorns and thistles.

It would be an extremely unsophisticated and literalist understanding of that statement to think that thorns and thistles were precisely the mode and extent of the curse that fell upon the ground. In the phrase "cursed is the ground because of you" there is the unstated potential for a vast amount of toil, difficulty, pain, and injury to man springing out of the ground.

Things entered into the natural realm as a result of Adam's sin that would never have been there apart from it and that have ever since been bad for man. Some are poisons. They damage a man's physical being if they are ingested, and they may cause death. Others have a different impact. There is something in their mysterious chemistry that causes them to loosen the grip that a man's will exerts on his own faculties—including his mind and his muscular and nervous responses. In some cases these cursed substances quickly carry a man where he has never previously been—into the realm of the demonic supernatural.

That is why it can accurately be stated that demons gain control through alcohol, narcotics, hallucinogens.

They may gain mental control, physical control, emotional control, or spiritual control. By taking these substances a man may undergo changes in consciousness that distort his capacity to judge right from wrong. He may find himself beginning to hold certain convictions about what is true and what is not true, contrary to the Scriptures, but be unaware that he has opened himself up to lies.

It is fairly common among young people to scorn alcohol and to embrace drugs. "Acid heads" do not admire "juice heads," or heavy drinkers. In a curiously perverse bit of reasoning, some young people justify their taking of drugs on the ground that their parents swill liquor. There *is* a distinction between them, but it is not the distinction commonly thought.

A recent report on medical research by Richard D. Lyons in the *Times* said, "Two New York biochemists reported today what they believe might be the long-sought scientific reason that alcohol can cause behavioral changes ranging from euphoria through drunkenness to hallucinations. Dr. Michael Collins and Gerald Cohen said that the body probably converted alcohol through a series of complicated steps to substances *chemically akin to morphine, peyote, and other opiates and hallucinogens.*"

So here in the biochemical laboratory researchers have begun to trace the hitherto hidden chemical relationships of alcohol and some of the most powerful narcotics and hallucinogens.

In addition to triggering hallucinations, these fearful chemicals sometimes induce psychoses. Of 114 LSD users hospitalized in one 18-month period at Bellevue Hospital in New York, 13 percent suffered *overwhelming panic,* 12 percent exhibited *uncontrolled violence,* nearly 9 percent had attempted *homicides or suicide.* One out of seven of them had to be sent for long-term mental hospitalization. "Half of those had no history of underlying psychiatric disorder," a physician reported. Some suffered acute schizophrenia. Several "withdrew from society into a totally solipsistic [self-contained] existence."

One report told of a boy on LSD who threw himself off a cliff because he believed he could fly.

The possibility of genetic damage has caused the National Foundation—March of Dimes, whose field of specialization is birth defects, to warn that "it is especially important that men and women in their reproductive years avoid using LSD."

In its assault on the body LSD penetrates to the very nucleus of the cells and attacks the chromosomes—tiny, threadlike particles of material buried in the nucleus of every cell which "transmit hereditary factors from one generation to the next." They carry the instructions that form new life.

At one medical school, eight young men, all users, volunteered blood samples for microscopic inspection. Six of the eight were found to have damaged—broken—chromosomes. Two of the six showed signs of "fatal chronic myelogenous leukemia," cancer of the blood. Chromosome damage represents a deep invasion of the inmost chambers of the body. Taking LSD may be one way to wreck a child before he's born.

The kind of chromosome damage caused by LSD can lead to an abnormality called the *cri-du-chat* syndrome, in which a baby cries like a cat, not like a human.

"The results of this chromosome damage may have a delayed effect that may not be in evidence until the second or third generation offspring," warned the renowned Dr. Howard A. Rusk, head of the Institute for Rehabilitation Medicine at the New York University Medical Center. Dr. Rusk found that the more immediate effects of the hallucinogens are "on the central nervous system and on the psychic and mental functions" and that these include a "possibility of permanent brain damage."

A dose or two of LSD and a child born to your granddaughter may come into the world crippled for life. What potency that is! All of the supposed benefits of drugs—the trips, the kicks, the highs, the hallucinations, the escape from reality, the illusion of increased powers—are transient and are offered in exchange for the chance to impose severe damage upon the user and deformities upon future generations.

What kind of an economy is it by which you pop a pill into your mouth now for a brief sensation and others have to pay and pay and pay through all the years of their lives? What is that to you? It is exactly what it would have been if one of your grandparents had, for the sake of some momentary transport, taken a drug so violent in its impact as to have caused you to be born with a gross deformity and to be penalized by it for life. It was your fortune to be born before the curse of drugs had begun to spread across our culture. You have no right to lay such a tax upon members of another generation.

Among the false religions Satan has devised there are some, including those centered on drugs, that feature quite sensational effects, including all kinds of interior fireworks shows and a dervish-like frenzy at times—creations of the special effects department of hell, intended to deceive. One thing these tribal religions do not do is to relieve hardship and suffering and poverty and ignorance. They perpetuate them. They intensify them, offering occasional soul flights as escapism. The *real conditions* under which the people live and labor are not changed, except for the worse.

Another common note is that of possession: the experience of being taken over by the will of the leader or by an outside force.

A reporter I know, a man of unusually forceful character and exceptionally strong will, came to me about three years ago and said that he had an opportunity to take LSD at a house gathering under the supervision of a man who had some experience at it. He asked if I thought he should go ahead. I explained why I thought it would be unwise.

About a week later he came by and said, "I want to tell you how wrong you were about that LSD. I tried it, and it was wonderful." He told something of the beautiful sensations he had experienced. I felt there was nothing I could say.

Two weeks later he came in quite a different mood. "I took another trip on LSD," he said, "and I thought I was losing my mind. I felt I was coming under the power of this guy who was guiding us. It got so bad I thought I was under his power completely, and the terrifying thing about it was I didn't know if I could ever get back. I'm not kidding, I didn't know if it was possible to come back."

Quite often, marijuana provides the initial introduction into the supernatural, serving as a gateway to deeper involvement later—either through other drugs or apart from drugs.

A college student in New York City said that it was only after taking marijuana that he became aware of certain hitherto unknown spirit beings he described as "my friends." He said frankly that he did not know whether they were good or evil spirits.

As to physical effects, medical observation has shown that "marijuana can hinder the individual's ability to function. Even small doses produce unsteadiness. Since *spatial perception, as well as coordination, is affected,* a marijuana user may be as dangerous as a drunk behind the wheel."

Tests have shown that an individual under the influence of marijuana *tends to lose his coordination,* yet he often has *a feeling of omnipotence.* So, while his actual efficiency goes down, his inclination to take risks shoots up, a dangerous combination.

One of Satan's most efficient instruments is the narcotics parlay: an innocent flirtation with marijuana now, a deadly alliance with heroin (or some other hard narcotic) later.

A study made in New York City in 1968 found that, out of 168 young people who had used marijuana, "at least 40 percent later began using heroin." People who wouldn't think of taking heroin will take marijuana, and some later graduate, for one reason or another, to more potent stuff.

A student friend at Yale who has watched undergraduates become involved with drugs—his older brother's use of marijuana led to a mental breakdown and hospitalization—put it this way:

"An airplane with a hundred seats is about to take off. The loudspeaker promises that the weather is fine and the view excellent, but it also warns the prospective passengers, 'In the middle of your flight, 40 of the seats will drop out of the bottom of the plane!' The prospective passengers face the question, 'Is this trip worth taking?' "

You may know four or five people, possibly more, who have used grass or something else who are still able to function perfectly well. That is right. Yet it may not be the case with you! Even if you knew 100 or 1,000, you cannot project that into a guarantee of a similar immunity for yourself.

The fact is that some people can't take the stuff without suffering damage, some can't take it without going out of their minds. If you're one of those, it doesn't make any difference how many people you know who can.

With all of these potent chemicals, the only sure thing is that if you don't bother with them, they won't bother you. *That is the only guarantee you have.* Everything else is playing a kind of Russian roulette with chemicals that may act like small charges of dynamite in your body or in your soul.

One girl in California took up marijuana at 17,

used it for three years, then tried LSD. She had a "good trip: We rolled on the floor and we laughed and the room filled up with gold fog and we swam through it."

A week later, she tried it again. She had a bad trip: "I began to shake and sweat and I felt like someone was pulling a band tight around my head." Three days later, "I was still trembling and crying all the time and everything still had that nightmare comic-strip look." When a reporter saw her nearly two years later, she had not taken any more LSD but she was still trembling and unable to work.

"Blow your mind" is a popular term that speaks of the mental effects of taking certain drugs.

The three words have a certain exactness in describing the explosively damaging effect upon the minds of some victims. The words are an invitation to disaster. You've got one mind. God gave it to you. It is the only one you will ever have, and Satan desires to take it from you, in part or in whole. Nothing could be more self-destructive than to "blow your mind." When you've blown that, buddy, you can never get a replacement.

If you wouldn't put a gun to your forehead and pull the trigger, you will be smart not to take something into your body that can devastate your brains.

A story in the *Times* by Paul L. Montgomery began: "Down the circular staircase in the airless basement of the city's Morgue on First Avenue, the day's consignment of drug-abuse fatalities reposed on stainless steel slabs—five young men between the ages of 18 and 21 who had been alive on Saturday and dead on Sunday."

Whether or not we are going to have a drug culture depends chiefly on what some young people decide to do now as they are confronted with the greatly increased availability of drugs in the nation.

Barry Farrell, in a *Life* essay on the great Woodstock Music and Art Festival of August 1969, spoke of "rock-dope" as a new "American religion" whose believers massed on the hillside at Bethel, New York, as though for a camp meeting of some "electro-chemical church."

It may, of course, be new to much of the United States, but it is a straight throwback to primitive, tribal religion.

This is brainwashing on the massive scale of a generation, not by any conspiracy of men, but by a deliberate and elaborate scheme of demons, promoted through the manipulation of fads, through the use of such catchwords and slogans as "Turn on, tune in, drop out."

We are made observers of the programmed destruction of a segment of the nation's young people, and the program is gaining speed and affecting greater numbers and most of us stand by not knowing quite what to make of it. What will it come to? Misery and sickness and addiction and untimely death for many. Despair and entrapment for others. Mental derangement in some degree for yet many more.

Drugs are useful to Satan as the opening wedge into false religion, but they are not at all necessary to its maintenance. Once drugs and hallucinogens have made a person subject to demon influence or control, their continued use is not necessary to the perpetuation of that state. Some individuals are so linked with evil spirits by the use of such chemicals that they are thereafter permanently under spiritual deception and are unable to receive spiritual truth. In Satan's economy they are on a fixed course for hell, with scant chance that they shall ever turn out of it.

Chapter 12

The Other Side
of the Ledger

The media, as discussed in an earlier chapter, have a wonderful and terrible power: They can grant, or deny, a public existence to individuals and movements by deciding to report on them or not to do so.

A man stands up on a platform and speaks. An audience hears him, but the media are not present. The next day what he said may be known to two or three times the number of people who heard him, but the event has no public existence beyond that limited circle. For millions, it never happened.

Another man stands up on a platform and speaks. An audience hears him, and the media are present —reporters, radio newsmen, television crews. Within hours the event may be made known, quite literally, to millions of people.

Certain people are recognized as "leaders" by the media, and what they say or do is extensively reported. A tremendous public distribution is thus afforded to the identity, the acts and ideas of these leaders.

In the whole context of American life, advocates of radical positions are granted a disproportionate share of total media time and attention.

In the winter and spring of 1970 many interruptions broke the normal pursuit of business on American college campuses. A stage was reached, after the Cambodian invasion and the shootings at Kent State University, at which finally hundreds of campuses were effectively put out of function.

That phenomenon was, rightly, carefully reported and the nation became wholly aware of it. But another phenomenon occurred in the late winter and early spring that was not widely reported in the media and was entirely ignored by the national press, though it caused the cessation of classes at campus after campus.

You probably never knew it was going on, yet it was surely one of the most remarkable episodes of this century in American higher education.

A kind of benign disruption of campus routine and classes came, spontaneously, as students at many campuses were suddenly and unaccountably affected by a strong desire to pray, to ask God to forgive them for the wrongs they had done to others. As many did so, there followed the welling up of a great joy that was outwardly expressed in thanksgiving, by word, prayer, and song.

At Asbury College in Kentucky, Hughes Auditorium became the focus of this unexpected advent of grace upon a bewildered generation. There was something utterly compelling about the atmosphere in that auditorium. Students were drawn to it, and those who came out after many hours could only say that God was in that place.

All classes were canceled. Day after day, night after night, students and faculty members, townspeople, high school youths went in and out of the auditorium for unplanned times of rejoicing in the Presence of God. The revival, which had no human leaders, ran on around the clock, continuously, for a week.

Personal enmities were healed, grudges forsaken,

old debts paid, lies and cheating confessed, among many other results. A television reporter from Lexington, Kentucky, told his audience that, in 34 years on the news beat, he had never seen anything that had impressed him as deeply as the event at Asbury College. A reporter I know visited the campus several weeks later. He told me that "the atmosphere there was wonderful: it was one big love-in." Yet it was a holy love-in, in which people did what was right, not what was wrong, where reconciliation was the keynote among students and adults.

Within a week the movement had spread to at least twenty other college campuses. Teams of students spread out across the country, from Florida to California, and up into Canada, to tell other students what had happened. More than 600 Asbury students went on the road, conveying the news to as many places as they could.

By any reasonable test, the shutting down of classes on college campuses because so many students are seized with a desire to *pray* is news. One definition of news is that which causes an interruption in the normal course, a break in the routine of life. And when prayer and confession and rejoicing meetings run on for days and nights, and when hundreds of students go out to tell others because they want to spread their joy, it is certainly news.

Yet it was largely ignored. It was covered, of course, by local media, newspaper and radio-television stations, but it never got a mention in the national press. As far as the consciousness of the mass American public was concerned, it might just as well not have happened.

The timing of the Asbury revival movement was spiritually significant. It began on February 3, just a few weeks before American higher education was to be thrust by national and world events into its most perplexed and unhappy spring, one that can reasonably be termed a season of student despair.

While division and confusion and despair were afflicting the college generation, along with such devices of the devil as false mysticism and drugs, God visited a campus to set in motion, by the gentle, prevailing Presence of the Holy Spirit, a movement of healing and reconciliation, of release and joy—a movement of such quiet force that it stilled the routine on campus after campus and compelled attention to first things.

It is not possible to tell how far the revival might have run if word of it had been communicated, while it was occurring, in the national media. The movement deserved something more than total nonrecognition.

A witch did not find it hard to get widespread publicity for her activities that spring. In its April 10, 1970, issue, *Life* devoted a three-page spread with five large pictures to Louise Huebner, "The Good Witch of the West," at a time when she was plugging her book, *Power Through Witchcraft.* When she made a self-promoting appearance in New York, the media readily showed up with cameras and microphones—in response to the desire of one witch to promote an occult book.

Certainly I do not want unfairly to criticize any one organ, and it is never conclusive to take a single instance and generalize from it. But it is perhaps an index of the present great imbalance that a national magazine had three pages for a report on the doings of one self-serving sorceress, including a picture of her surrounded by high school students, but none for a quite extraordinary movement, involving at least forty campuses and 600 students who traveled as itinerant heralds of the good news that God is alive and is acting in our generation.

This is not a summons to a hear-no-evil, see-no-evil, speak-no-evil complacency. That would be dangerous. It is no call for censorship. When that arises, liberty dies. It is an appeal, in a situation of virtually unlimited liberty, for discrimination, restraint, and especially for a balancing of the ledger so that the red ink of social distress will not get so nearly all of the attention.

Every day the mass media inject into the mainstream of American life and thought certain influences—events, personalities, ideas. If these daily injections pump in so much more of what contributes to the ill-being of a society than of what contributes to its well-being, accentuating the problems while minimizing the solutions, then trouble has an unusual opportunity to feed on trouble.

Charter of Freedom

At the Radcliffe commencement in 1968, Miss Susannah H. Wood prayed:

"We do not feel like a cool, swinging generation—we are eaten up inside by an intensity that we cannot name.

"Help us to prepare a kind of renaissance in our public and private lives. Let there be born in us a strange joy, that will help us to live and to die and to remake the soul of our time."

Let there be born in us a strange joy!

There is a joy that is beyond all the power of words to catch. When David brought the ark of God to Jerusalem, he was filled with great joy. "And David danced before the Lord with all his might. . . . So David and all the house of Israel brought up the ark of the Lord with shouting, and with the sound of the trumpet. As the ark of the Lord came into the city of David, Michal, Saul's daughter looked through a window, and saw King David *leaping and dancing* before the Lord" (2 Samuel 6:14-16).

Religious processions are supposed to be solemn affairs and kings ought to bear themselves as though they had been starched, and David's wife came out to scold David for what seemed to her an unseemly display of religious hilarity. But David said to her, "It was before the Lord, who chose me above your father and above all his house, to appoint me ruler over the people of the Lord . . . therefore I will celebrate before the Lord" (2 Samuel 6:21, NAS).

"I will celebrate before the Lord."

David had a joy in him that day that could not be contained. It was not that he thought he ought to dance. He had so much joy in his heart that it had to come out at his feet.

The kind of joy David had that day comes only out of a close identification with the purposes of God—an identification in which you are given something bigger to do than you can possibly do on your own, and on which you risk everything. The joy comes as you see God intervening to make possible the impossible.

When it is done, you know absolutely that if God had not acted, it would not have been done. The joy of David was the joy of seeing God in action. It was also the joy of knowing God.

To experience that kind of joy, a man has got to take radical action. Not the kind of radical action that is causing so much commotion lately, but action that is just as radical in a different direction.

Gideon is a wonderful example. God called Gideon to be the leader of the Jewish people at a time when they were living under extreme oppression by heathen nations, so that they made for themselves "dens which are in the mountains and the caves" and hid in them (Judges 6:2b,3).

The situation was terrible. How was it going to be changed? The first thing God told Gideon to do was to act against his own father's false gods by tearing them down. (Judges 6:25)

Gideon started by destroying the false altars in his own backyard. It was the beginning of a career that was shortly to see him put the enemies of Israel to rout and to bring immense relief to the Jews.

It was a good place to start. It may be where you should start. The God of Israel demands exclusive devotion to Himself, and He commands us to have "no other gods." What have you got—what books, what images, what occult devices, what medals or anything else—that represent religion or divination apart from the God of Israel? Whatever it is, in articles or in practices, it is a sign of allegiance to a false god, and the Scriptures require you to get rid of it.

Gideon acted against the religious tradition of his family and against the religious practices of the town, but notice this: The action that Gideon took was not his *own* idea of what should be done about the situation that confronted him. It wasn't even something that he wanted to do. It was something that he did not want to do. He did it because God told him to do it. He took specific action according to nothing but the Word of God.

Gideon was a radical, but he was a radical for God. He went out against a huge enemy army with 300 men, armed only with trumpets and empty jars and torches. There wasn't a sword among them. They were outnumbered by 450 to one. Gideon had a secret weapon: the promise of God to act on Israel's behalf at the critical moment. The whole enemy army was put to utter rout, and Israel was delivered from years of intense oppression.

God has something bigger for you to do than you can possibly do. That was true with David, with Gideon, with Moses. What God gives you to do will absolutely, somewhere in its course, require His direct intervention if the thing is to be done. When you see God in action, doing the impossible through you, you will taste joy and you may know something about the way David felt when he brought the ark into Jerusalem. Your part is faith.

What is faith? The best definition I know is: Faith is a *voluntary act* of trust in God.

Another is: "Now faith is the assurance of things hoped for, the conviction of things not seen" (Hebrews 11:1, NAS).

Gideon trusted the invisible God to come into visible action, and he staked everything on it. That is faith.

Faith, as a basis for life, is radically different from any other. Faith risks everything on the veracity of God.

When a man does that, God acts on his behalf. Oswald Chambers put it this way: "When we choose deliberately to obey Him, then He will tax the remotest star and the last grain of sand to assist us with all His almighty power."

No Divided Loyalties

A man must not be divided in faith:

"No one can serve two masters; for either he will hate the one and love the other, or he will hold to the one and despise the other. You cannot serve God and mammon," Jesus said in the Sermon on the Mount.

"For this reason I say to you, do not be anxious for your life, as to what you shall eat, or what you shall drink; nor for your body, as to what you shall put on. Is not life more than food, and the body than clothing? Look at the birds of the air, that they do not sow, neither do they reap, nor gather into barns; and yet your heavenly Father feeds them. Are you not worth much more than they?

"Therefore do not be anxious for tomorrow; for tomorrow will care for itself. Each day has enough trouble of its own" (Matthew 6:24-26, 34, NAS).

This is a *charter of freedom* because it is true, and God will back it up entirely in your experience as you make it the basis of life.

Since most men have to look out for themselves to be sure they get enough of what they want and need, they are not free because they are obligated to be the source of their own supply. But as God adds all these things to a man as the man lives for Him, a man is free. God is the source of his supply.

The failure of materialism as a life cause is its total incapacity to meet or to answer the ultimate questions. It is mute on those things. It is embarrassed by them.

As a way of life, materialism takes what is only a means and makes it into an end. It is idolatry. I recently saw a large sign in an automobile dealer's window: "Buick—Something To Believe In." Israel had its golden calf; we've got the Buick.

Yet to reject materialism may be to incur binding poverty that makes life hard and narrow and bitter. To break with materialism is a step, but it is not enough. The spiritual void is still there.

It is not until God is at the center of a man's life that spiritual and material things fall into their right relationship.

God acts in response to faith. George Mueller, the great British man of faith, took in orphans by the hundreds, loved them, refused ever to tell anyone of his needs, and trusted God for all the provisions necessary for all those children.

One morning the larder was absolutely bare. The children had come down for breakfast and were seated at the tables. Mueller, knowing there was nothing for them *yet,* bowed his head and gave thanks to God for the food that was about to be set before the children for breakfast—from he knew not where—and as he raised his head from the prayer, a loud knocking came at the door. A baker was there with a load of sweet bread and milk.

A young woman named Lettie Cowman, an ardent believer, conceived a great desire to provide the Scriptures for the people of the Orient. She took it to God in earnest prayer and bought a small notebook in which to enter contributions for the purpose. The first entry was 25 cents. Before many years had passed, $5 million had passed through her hands and the Scriptures had poured into the Orient. It was "impossible," but she did it by faith. She tapped the infinite resources of God.

Faith does not work, I hasten to add, as a principle of self-service nor as a warrant for a life of idle ease. That perverts the promise. The point is not that God is going to serve you. You must serve God and, as you do that, He *will* provide for you. "I have been young, and now am old," David declared, "yet I have not seen the righteous forsaken, nor his children begging bread" (Psalm 37:25). One translation of Matthew 6:33 says of material things, "God will give them to you gladly if you put Him first in your life."

My own experience of trusting God for my needs began in a small way. I was in the Army, had just embarked on the life of faith before being drafted, and I needed to take a bus to the other side of Baltimore, but did not have a nickel. "Be careful [anxious] for nothing," the Bible says, "but in everything by prayer and supplication with thanksgiving let your requests be made known to God" (Philippians 4:6). Faith rose and I just told the Lord silently that I needed bus fare two ways. As soon as I did, I was filled with assurance that the Lord would provide it.

Half an hour later He did, through the man in the bunk next to me who decided that he should take half a dollar out of his pocket and hand it to me. That half-dollar made me happier at that moment than $10 could have some other time.

The Bible is our charter of freedom from want. It is also our charter of freedom from sin.

Sin is a problem, because no one caught in it is free. "Every one who commits sin is a slave to sin" (John 8:34). That is plain enough, and if you are honest, you know it is true. You sin because you don't have the strength or the power not to, even though you know it's wrong.

Every once in a while you hear people say they live by the Ten Commandments or the Sermon on the Mount, or both. That is nonsense. No man can live by either, if he tries to live by them as rules. Most people who say that can't name the commandments anyway, and they could not quote six verses from the Sermon on the Mount.

It takes new life to live by God's standards. It takes power to live above the power of sin.

My own experience of this new life, and the power over sin and freedom from it, began shortly after I read these wonderful words:

"He was in the world, and the world was made by Him, and the world knew Him not. He came unto His own, and His own received Him not.

"But as many as received Him, to them gave He *power to become the sons of God,* even to them that believe on His name, who were born, not of blood, nor of the will of the flesh, nor of the will of man, but of God" (John 1:10-13).

When I first saw those words, they hit me with considerable force. I knew that I was not a son of God, but the Bible said God was able to give me "power to become a son of God." About three days later I received that power.

Jesus Christ came into my life, and sin went out of my life. That is not to say that I never sinned again, but the power that sin had held over me, despite my best efforts to overcome it, was broken. Sin could no longer compel me to do its bidding. As long as you lack power over sin, you are not free.

No matter how much of a hold sin has on your life, that situation can be suddenly and utterly reversed. There is entire forgiveness with God because the blood of Jesus Christ has fully atoned for sin. God sets a believer in a new relationship to temptation—above it, not under it.

Surprised by Joy

The transformation that comes with forgiveness of sins brings a new joy. C. S. Lewis, the English writer, who knew this transformation in his own experience, wrote a book about it. He called it *Surprised by Joy.*

The Apostle Paul writes, "Now the deeds of the flesh are evident, which are: immorality, impurity, sensuality, idolatry, sorcery, enmities, strife, jealousy, outbursts of anger, disputes, dissensions, factions, envyings, drunkenness, carousings, and things like these, of which I forewarn you just as I have forewarned you that those who practice such things shall not inherit the kingdom of God" (Galatians 5:19-21, NAS).

It may be that you are habitually involved in one or more of these things. If so, you have yet to be transformed.

The Bible very clearly explains that "That which is born of the flesh is flesh, and that which is born of the Spirit is spirit" (John 3:6).

If you have been born of the flesh only—that is, by your natural parents—then you *are* flesh, and it is natural that you would be in some of these things. When you are born of the Spirit—that is, born of God, and given power to become a son of God—you will be absolutely new. You will be a different person. That difference will not only surprise other people, it will surprise you.

A young law student named Charles Grandison Finney became America's foremost revivalist near the time of the Civil War. His exposure to the truths of the Bible brought Finney to the consciousness that he was a sinner and that he "needed a great change in my inward state."

God met him at the point of his need and Finney was soon brought to a living faith in Jesus Christ: "I found that my mind had become most wonderfully quiet and peaceful," he wrote of his experience. "I walked quietly toward the village, and so perfectly quiet was my mind that it seemed as if all nature listened." His slate had been wiped clean through the blood of Jesus Christ.

This was the start of Finney's lifelong experience with God, but there was yet another transaction—an outpouring of the Holy Spirit upon him: "The Holy Spirit descended upon me in a manner that seemed to go through me body and soul . . . Indeed this seemed to come in waves and waves of liquid love. It seemed like the very breath of God. No words can express the wonderful love that was shed abroad in my heart. I wept aloud with joy and love; and I do not know but I should say, I literally bellowed out the unutterable gushings of my heart.

"When J awoke in the morning the sun had risen, and was pouring a clear light into my room. . . . Instantly the baptism that I had received the night before returned upon me in the same manner. I arose upon my knees in the bed and wept aloud with joy."

Finney soon "sallied forth from the office to converse with those whom I should meet about their souls," and he did so with wonderfully good effect. He found that young people were "converted one after another with great rapidity" and that the work of the Holy Spirit "spread among all classes, and extended . . . not only through the village, but out of the village in every direction."

Finney had no formal theological education: "When I first began to preach, and for some 12 years of my earliest ministry, I wrote not a word, and was most commonly obliged to preach without any preparation whatever, except what I got in prayer . . . I preached out of doors; I preached in barns; I preached in schoolhouses; and a glorious revival spread all over that region of the country." His autobiography, chiefly a report on revivals, is one of the most thrilling accounts of modern Christian history.

Some people suppose that God desires a dull, pleasureless, rigorous life for man, full of petty restrictions. That is far from the truth. John Wesley put it well when he said, "Sour godliness is the devil's religion."

God has filled the earth with things that give great and lawful pleasure to man. He is the author of happiness. No true pleasure is possible apart from Him. "Every good gift and perfect gift is from above, . . . from the Father of lights" (James 1:17).

"No good thing does He [the Lord] withhold from those who walk uprightly" (Psalm 84:11, NAS). "Thou wilt make known to me the path of life; in Thy presence is fullness of joy; in Thy right hand there are pleasures forever" (Psalm 16:11, NAS).

God wants us to have pleasure, now and throughout eternity, but he is not willing that our pleasure be gained at anyone else's sorrow and expense. He is not willing that our pleasure be gained at our own sorrow and expense.

Satan has never been responsible for the creation of any true pleasure. His role is to take the pleasures created by God and to pervert them into that which leads to the destruction of man.

Satan doesn't have any interest in pleasure for humans, except as a means of bringing them pain. He uses pleasure as a convenient tactic in his strategy to increase human misery. That is his sole interest in pleasure.

Satan presses *self-gratification* upon man. He will always counsel a man to act on appetites, impulses, desires—without considering the long-range effects. That is one of the chief lines of his propaganda, and you see it everywhere. Are you angry? Are you jealous? Do you have lust? Are you consumed with ambition? Go ahead, he urges, don't wait; act on these *now*.

The promptings of immediate self-gratification, without regard to consequences, are an echo of Satan's counsel to the woman in the garden.

In the final analysis you are going to have to take God's Word or Satan's.

The pot-sex-protest mode that Satan is increasingly foisting on us, is not the way to liberty that it claims to be. It is the way to bondage, destruction, and death.

God wants young people, and people generally, to have the real thing, not Satan's terrible counterfeits.

To get to this ultimate reality, a personal encounter with Jesus Christ Himself through the Holy Spirit, an experience of His love and supernatural power that cannot be argued away, you must be willing to make a clean break with sin and with all demonic substitutes, and give yourself radically to God.

To be free, find out what God wants you to do and do it.

When you discover the joy that only God can give, your own life will be wonderfully changed and you will be able to help remake the soul of our time in ways of which you cannot now even guess.

"For you shall go out in joy, and be led forth in peace. The mountains and the hills shall break forth before you into singing, and all the trees of the field shall clap their hands" (Isaiah 55:12).

If you have never heard the mountains singing, or seen the trees of the field clapping their hands, do not think because of that that they don't. Ask God to open your ears so you may hear it, and your eyes so you may see it, because, though few men ever know it, they do, my friend, they do.